Alfred Essa
Artificial Intelligence

AI Essentials for Leaders

Edited by
Alfred Essa and Teresa Martín-Retortillo

Alfred Essa

Artificial Intelligence

Shaping the Future of Innovation

DE GRUYTER

ISBN 978-3-11-158238-2
e-ISBN (PDF) 978-3-11-158354-9
e-ISBN (EPUB) 978-3-11-158411-9
ISSN 2944-2540

Library of Congress Control Number: 2025943011

Bibliographic information published by the Deutsche Nationalbibliothek
The Deutsche Nationalbibliothek lists this publication in the Deutsche Nationalbibliografie;
detailed bibliographic data are available on the Internet at http://dnb.dnb.de.

For Robert Ubell,
a constant friend and fellow traveler

Preface

Artificial intelligence is no longer on the horizon—it is already reshaping markets and transforming how we work, learn, and grow. Yet many organizations still treat AI as a future concern. Forward-thinking leaders understand that the groundwork for lasting advantage must be laid now. History shows that transformative technologies rarely yield immediate returns: capabilities take time to build, ramp-up is steep, and the gap between early adopters and laggards widens quickly. The question is no longer whether AI will transform organizations—it is whether they will invest early enough to seize the opportunity before it slips away.

This book is written for decision-makers who need to understand AI's capabilities and limitations without getting lost in technical jargon. While some formulas and code snippets appear, they're presented gently to support intuition, not overwhelm. The focus is on clear explanations of how AI systems work, what they can and cannot do, and how to think strategically about their use in organizational contexts.

A central thesis of this book is that while much attention centers on AI technology itself—especially foundation models—the greatest opportunities lie in practical applications. As Andrew Ng notes, in examining the AI stack from semiconductors and cloud infrastructure through foundation models to applications, it's at the application layer where most organizations will find their competitive edge (Ng, 2024). This book equips readers with the understanding needed to lead organizations that build and deploy these applications, regardless of technical background.

The goal is to help readers develop an *entrepreneurial mindset* toward AI—whether leading a startup, an established enterprise, a non-profit, or a government agency. This means seeing beyond the hype to identify concrete opportunities, understanding the technology well enough to make informed decisions, and approaching implementation with both ambition and appropriate caution. This balanced approach is essential for navigating the complex landscape of AI implementation, where both excessive skepticism and uncritical enthusiasm can lead to strategic missteps.

One of the most important insights is that AI is not a monolith but a *system of interconnected components*. Just as understanding an automobile doesn't require deep knowledge of combustion engines but does require knowing how the steering wheel connects to the chassis and how these interconnections enable functional control of the vehicle, effective AI leadership demands an understanding of how different components work together—even if the technical details are left to specialists. This systems view enables smarter decisions and avoids costly investments in poorly integrated or risky technologies.

https://doi.org/10.1515/9783111583549-203

One key to understanding AI is recognizing the hierarchy of fields that make up the broader system. At the top sits Artificial Intelligence, the broad ambition of building machines capable of intelligent behavior. Within AI, Machine Learning focuses on systems that learn patterns from data rather than relying on fixed instructions. Deep Learning, in turn, is a subset of Machine Learning that uses layered neural networks to process complex inputs like images, text, and speech. Generative AI builds on Deep Learning by creating new content—writing text, composing music, generating images—rather than simply making predictions. Figure 1 below illustrates this nested structure and provides a roadmap for how the sections of this book fit together.

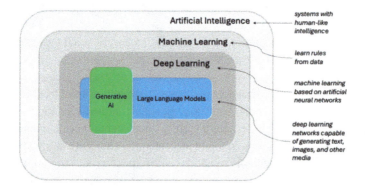

Figure 1: Hierarchical Depiction of AI Fields. The relationship between Artificial Intelligence, Machine Learning, Deep Learning, and Generative AI. Each layer represents a specialization of the broader field above it. This nested structure provides the conceptual roadmap for the AI-specific technical sections of the book.

With this structure in mind, the book is organized into six parts, each building on the last to offer a focused understanding of AI and its applications, using clear explanations and real-world case studies.

How This Book Is Organized

– **Part I: AI as Innovation** examines artificial intelligence as a general purpose technology that, like electricity or the internet, is transforming every sector of the economy. Readers will learn why new technologies often experience a "productivity paradox"—where benefits lag behind adoption—and how to build an innovation culture that overcomes this challenge. This section provides the strategic context for everything that follows.

- **Part II: Computation** introduces the basic mechanics of computing, including how algorithms and computer architectures process information. These fundamentals help distinguish genuine technical constraints from limitations that clever engineering might solve.
- **Part III: Machine Learning** shifts from traditional programming to systems that learn from data. Through case studies in classification and regression, readers will see how organizations can use data to predict outcomes and make better decisions. The section emphasizes how simple, transparent models can deliver substantial value with lower cost and complexity than advanced alternatives.
- **Part IV: Deep Learning** explains the breakthrough technology behind recent AI advances. Using intuitive analogies rather than mathematics, this part clarifies how neural networks process information layer by layer to recognize patterns in data. This knowledge is essential for understanding both the capabilities and limitations of modern AI systems.
- **Part V: Generative AI** explores the systems behind tools like ChatGPT, Claude, and DeepSeek. This section explains how foundation models, expert models, and AI agents work together as an integrated system, each addressing different challenges. These chapters help distinguish between different types of AI tools and identify which are appropriate for specific applications.
- **Part VI: Risk** examines why AI systems fail and how to manage those risks effectively. This is perhaps the most important section of the book. The chapters on risk apply established frameworks from complex systems theory to help identify potential failure points before they cause problems. Readers will learn how multi-agent AI systems mirror human organizational failures, why certain AI architectures are prone to "normal accidents" due to their interactive complexity and tight coupling, and how risks fundamentally transform when AI systems move from generating information to taking autonomous action. This section equips readers with practical approaches to design more reliable AI systems through organizational thinking, systemic resilience, and appropriate governance frameworks.

The Leader's Approach to AI

Throughout the book, five key principles are emphasized for leaders navigating the AI era:

- First, focus on applications, not just technology. While understanding foundation models is useful, the greatest opportunities lie in solving specific business problems through targeted applications.

- Second, treat AI as a system, not a black box. Knowing how foundation models, expert models, and agents interact leads to better decisions about adoption and implementation.
- Third, understand the progression in capability from machine learning to deep learning to generative AI. Each layer builds on the last, enabling a shift from prediction to content generation. Knowing where a technology fits helps set realistic expectations and avoid mismatches between problems and tools.
- Fourth, adopt an entrepreneurial mindset that balances ambition with pragmatism. The biggest gains will come from systematic experimentation—not massive, one-off projects, but focused initiatives with clear objectives.
- Fifth, view risk systemically, not just at the component level. Failures often arise from interactions among parts. Leaders must develop organizational thinking around AI risk, build oversight frameworks, and decide which applications are worth pursuing. As AI systems evolve from passive to active roles, this mindset becomes critical.

Beyond the Book: Additional Resources

While the book is designed for non-technical readers, many may wish to go deeper. Our website (https://ai-innov.org) offers supplementary material—including advanced mathematical treatments and code examples—for hands-on experimentation. As new technologies emerge, we'll update the site to keep readers current.

For educators, we provide slides, discussion prompts, and projects to support classroom use and applied learning. These will be made available at the same website.

What's Not in the Book

Several areas are intentionally not addressed in this book:
- **Artificial General Intelligence (AGI)**: Despite significant attention in media and research circles, there is no consensus on what AGI actually means or how it might be achieved. Rather than speculate on paths toward human-like artificial intelligence, this book focuses on the concrete capabilities and limitations of current systems.
- **Quantum Computing for AI**: Although quantum computing may eventually revolutionize certain AI applications, the technology remains largely experimental. This book emphasizes approaches that can deliver value today rather than technologies that may be years or decades from practical implementation.

–   **AI as an Existential Risk**: While debates about AI's potential to pose catastrophic or existential risks have gained prominence, the immediate focus for most organizations is understanding and implementing AI responsibly in the near term. This book prioritizes practical guidance over speculative long-term scenarios.

It's important to note that this book is part of a planned series. Many topics not covered in depth here will be addressed in upcoming volumes. For readers interested in a deeper exploration of how AI transforms business strategy, I recommend the companion volume *Artificial Intelligence: Rethinking Business Strategy* by Teresa Martín-Retortillo (De Gruyter, 2026). This second book in our "AI Essentials for Leaders" series examines how business leaders can navigate the complex decision landscape, identify which strategic principles still apply, and understand the relevant value drivers in the AI era. Each book in the series is designed to provide focused, actionable insights on specific aspects of AI implementation and strategy, building a comprehensive resource for leaders navigating the AI landscape.

Taking the First Steps Toward AI Transformation

The coming years will separate organizations that merely use AI from those that lead with it. This book aims to help readers join the latter—not by turning them into technical experts, but by giving them the conceptual tools to lead with confidence in an AI-powered world.

The future belongs to leaders who understand both the potential and the practical realities of artificial intelligence. Let's begin.

Contents

Part III: **Machine Learning**

Part IV: **Deep Learning**

Part V: **Generative AI**

Part VI: **Risk**

Part I: **Innovation**

1 Innovation Dynamics: AI's Transformative Potential

> You can see the computer age everywhere but in the productivity statistics.
> —Robert Solow

Throughout history, a small number of breakthrough technologies have reshaped how economies function and how societies operate. These innovations don't just solve one problem or improve one industry—they transform nearly everything they touch. The steam engine, for instance, didn't just power factories; it launched the Industrial Revolution. Electricity didn't just light homes; it fundamentally rewired modern civilization.

Economists refer to these far-reaching innovations as **general purpose technologies**, or **GPTs**. Unlike narrow technologies, GPTs provide broad capabilities that reach across many sectors of the economy. They catalyze cascading innovations and change the rules of what is possible. They are rare, but when they appear, they change history.

Artificial intelligence is now widely recognized by economists as a general purpose technology. Its rapid development, broad range of applications, and growing impact across industries make it comparable to earlier breakthroughs like electricity and the internet. For leaders in business, government, and non-profits, understanding AI as a general purpose technology provides essential context for navigating the changes ahead.

This chapter explores what makes a technology "general purpose," briefly looks at historical examples of GPTs, presents the case for AI as the latest member of this group, and offers guidance on how organizations can prepare for the changes it will bring.

1.1 What Is a General Purpose Technology?

A general purpose technology is more than just a useful innovation—it's a breakthrough that reshapes the entire global economy. Economists Timothy Bresnahan and Manuel Trajtenberg introduced the term in 1995 to describe technologies that act as engines of growth by driving change across many sectors, not just one (Bresnahan and Trajtenberg, 1995). Once they gain traction, GPTs become the *prime movers* of economic productivity and technology innovation.

GPTs enable entire ecosystems of innovation. What makes GPTs so powerful is that they don't just make existing tasks more efficient. They allow people and organizations to do things that weren't previously possible. They change how we organize businesses, build cities, and live our daily lives.

https://doi.org/10.1515/9783111583549-002

The Three Essential Characteristics of GPTs

What elevates a technology from simply "important" to truly "general purpose"? Economists have identified three key characteristics that define genuine GPTs:

Pervasiveness
A true general purpose technology is *pervasive*, not limited to one sector or one nation. It spreads across the economy, finding uses in many different settings. Electricity began with a few specialized applications but soon powered factories, homes, offices, farms, and transportation. Computing and the Internet started in academia and the military, but now play a role in nearly every industry. This kind of broad, cross-cutting adoption is what defines a GPT—not as a niche tool, but as a foundational capability that almost everyone eventually relies on.

Continuous Improvement
General purpose technologies don't stand still—*improvements accelerate over time*, becoming more powerful, efficient, and affordable. This progress makes them increasingly useful and accessible. Computing, for example, has advanced at an extraordinary pace. A key driver of this has been Moore's Law—the observation that the number of transistors on a microchip doubles roughly every two years, leading to exponential increases in computing power and efficiency. This steady, compounding progress has made modern devices vastly more capable and far less expensive than early computers. Driven by decades of innovation in semiconductor technology—from bulky transistors to today's dense, high-speed chips—computing has evolved rapidly. As a GPT evolves, its growing power and reach expand its impact across the economy.

Innovation Catalyst
Most importantly, a true general purpose technology sparks *cascading innovations*. These are waves of new ideas that build on each other. They also cross boundaries between industries and sectors. The Internet is a clear example—it led to web browsers, search engines, e-commerce, social media, and much more. Each of these, in turn, enabled further breakthroughs: online advertising transformed marketing, cloud computing reshaped software delivery, and mobile apps changed how people interact with businesses and each other. These ripple effects are what make GPTs so transformative. When a technology is widely adopted, steadily improves, and fuels cascading innovations, it has the defining traits of a GPT—one that drives deep and lasting change across the economy and society (Figure 1.1).

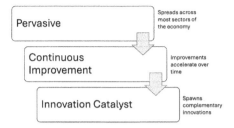

Figure 1.1: Three Primary Characteristics of General Purpose Technologies. GPTs are defined by their pervasiveness across multiple sectors, their capacity for continuous improvement over time, and their ability to generate cascading innovations that spawn new applications and industries. These interconnected characteristics distinguish GPTs from ordinary technologies and explain their transformative economic impact.

The Steam Engine (18th Century)

The steam engine emerged in the early 18th century as one of the first true general purpose technologies. It provided controllable power independent of geography, revolutionizing manufacturing by freeing production from natural power sources. Beyond merely accelerating existing processes, steam power fundamentally transformed industrial organization, enabling larger factories, spawning new industries, and reshaping cities. Steam-powered transportation connected previously isolated markets, dramatically reducing costs. The technology's transformative impact unfolded over more than a century, demonstrating how GPTs take time to reshape economies and how early adopters gain sustained advantages.

Electricity (Late 19th–Early 20th Century)

Electricity emerged as a transformative GPT in the late 19th century, with widespread adoption accelerating in the early 20th century. In manufacturing, distributed electric motors replaced centralized steam power systems, allowing factories to reorganize their layouts for dramatically improved efficiency. Beyond industrial applications, electricity enabled countless new products and services—from home appliances to telecommunications. However, the full productivity benefits weren't immediate. As historian Paul David noted, major productivity gains didn't materialize until the 1920s, decades after introduction (David, 1990). Organizations that merely replaced steam engines with electric motors saw modest improvements, while those who redesigned their operations around electricity's unique capabilities achieved transformative results—illustrating the crucial role of complementary innovations and organizational changes in realizing a GPT's full value.

Internal Combustion Engine (20th Century)

The internal combustion engine revolutionized 20th-century economies by powering automobiles, aircraft, and agricultural machinery—fundamentally transforming mobility, freight transport, and industrial efficiency. Its impact reached far beyond transportation, reshaping human geography through suburban development and car-centric urban planning. The technology catalyzed entirely new business ecosystems, from automobile manufacturing giants that standardized mass production to nationwide networks of fueling stations, repair facilities, and tourist accommodations. Like other GPTs, its transformative potential materialized gradually, enabled by complementary innovations including highway systems, gasoline distribution networks, and entirely new retail and service industries—all collectively reshaping economic structures and daily life patterns.

Computers and the Internet (Digital Age)

Computers and the internet represent a powerful pairing of general purpose technologies that define our current Information Age. Computing evolved from specialized calculation tools to ubiquitous devices that permeate nearly every economic sector, with exponential improvements in price-performance driven by Moore's Law. The internet transformed this computing foundation into a global information and coordination network, enabling e-commerce, search engines, digital media, and social networks that have revolutionized how we work, shop, learn, and connect.

Despite their eventual impact, productivity gains initially lagged behind technology adoption. Robert Solow famously noted in the 1980s: "You can see the computer age everywhere but in the productivity statistics (Solow, 1987)." Significant economic benefits emerged only after organizations developed complementary skills, processes, and business models—reinforcing the pattern seen with previous GPTs that technological capability alone isn't sufficient without corresponding organizational adaptation. This historical pattern provides valuable perspective as we examine AI's emergence as the next transformative general purpose technology (Figure 1.2).

1.2 AI: The Next General Purpose Technology

Today, artificial intelligence stands poised to join the elite group of general purpose technologies that have reshaped our world. The evidence is increasingly compelling that AI exhibits all three hallmark characteristics of a true GPT.

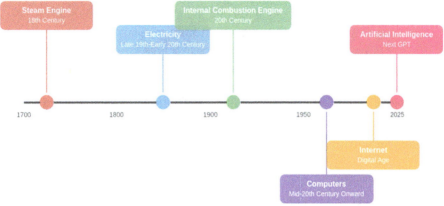

Figure 1.2: Evolution of General Purpose Technologies (GPTs). The timeline illustrates the chronological development of transformative technologies from the Steam Engine to Electricity, the Internal Combustion Engine, and the digital revolution marked by Computers and the Internet. The timeline concludes with Artificial Intelligence as the emerging next-generation GPT.

Broad Applicability Across Sectors

AI represents a toolkit with applications spanning virtually every economic sector. In healthcare, it enhances diagnostics and drug discovery; in finance, it powers trading algorithms and fraud detection; in manufacturing, it enables predictive maintenance and automation; while in creative fields, it augments design and content creation capabilities. This widespread cross-sector adoption demonstrates the pervasiveness characteristic of true general purpose technologies, with few industries remaining untouched by its transformative potential.

Continuous and Rapid Improvement

AI capabilities are advancing at a remarkable pace, conquering tasks previously considered impossible while becoming simultaneously more accessible and affordable. Training advanced models grows increasingly efficient, while cloud-based services democratize access to sophisticated capabilities without requiring specialized expertise. The technology exhibits positive feedback loops—improving through use as algorithms become more efficient and data accumulates—mirroring the pattern of continuous improvement seen in previous GPTs while steadily reducing costs for all users.

Catalyst for Further Innovation

Most significantly, AI functions as a platform enabling cascading innovations across domains. New drug discovery methods identify compounds human researchers might overlook, creative tools augment design processes, and smart systems optimize previously unmanageable complex operations. AI's combinatorial power with complementary technologies—from IoT sensors providing data to robotics executing physical tasks—creates entirely new possibilities and application categories. This "innovation-spawning" effect provides perhaps the strongest evidence of AI's status as a genuine general purpose technology—a foundation supporting entirely new categories of tools and services.

Expert Perspectives on AI as a GPT

Leading voices increasingly recognize AI's GPT status. AI pioneer Andrew Ng characterizes it as "the new electricity," predicting sector-wide transformation paralleling electrification (Ng, 2024). Economists studying technological change note AI's fulfillment of key GPT criteria—"pervasiveness, continuous improvement, and innovation spawning"—and forecast economic impact comparable to electricity or internal combustion engines. For business leaders, this framing provides crucial strategic context, suggesting not a passing trend but a fundamental capability shift driving decades of change.

However, if history guides us, realizing this new GPT's full potential won't happen automatically or immediately—bringing us to the *productivity paradox* typically accompanying general purpose technology introductions.

1.3 The Productivity Paradox: Why GPT Benefits Take Time

One of the most perplexing aspects of general purpose technologies is that their economic benefits often arrive much later than their technological capabilities. This delayed impact—known as the *productivity paradox*—has been observed with previous GPTs and is likely to happen with AI as well.

The Historical Pattern: Initial Investment, Delayed Returns

When a revolutionary technology appears, one might expect productivity and economic performance to jump immediately. Interestingly, the opposite often happens in the short term.

This pattern was famously observed with computers. Despite massive investments in computing technology throughout the 1970s and 1980s, productivity growth remained sluggish. It wasn't until the late 1990s—decades after the introduction of business computing—that a surge in productivity arrived that many economists attributed to information technology.

Similar patterns appeared with earlier GPTs. The big productivity gains from electrification didn't fully materialize until the 1920s, even though electric motors had been introduced in the 1880s. Factories that installed electric motors but maintained their old production layouts (designed for steam power) saw minimal improvement. Only when they completely redesigned their operations to leverage electricity's unique capabilities did the productivity revolution occur.

The Productivity J-Curve

Economist Erik Brynjolfsson has studied this phenomenon extensively, describing it as the "productivity J-Curve" (Brynjolfsson et al., 2019). When a GPT is first introduced, measured productivity often grows slowly or even dips before eventually accelerating—creating a J-shaped trajectory (Figure 1.3).

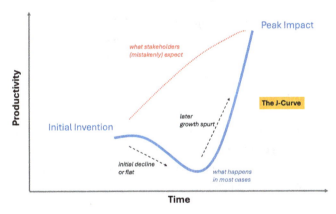

Figure 1.3: The Productivity J-Curve. This diagram illustrates how GPTs may initially show flat or even declining measured productivity before delivering accelerated returns once complementary innovations and organizational changes mature. Stakeholders mistakenly expect immediate returns.

Why does this happen? Because initially, organizations invest substantial resources in the new technology and in learning how to use it, but haven't yet developed the complementary innovations, skills, and organizational changes needed to fully exploit it. During this period, much of the investment goes into intangible, un-measured outputs (learning, reorganizing, experimenting) that don't immediately show up in productivity statistics.

Once those complementary changes are in place, however, productivity can take off dramatically—hence the steep upward curve of the "J" after its initial flat or downward segment.

AI's Current Productivity Paradox

We appear to be experiencing this same dynamic with artificial intelligence. In recent years, AI has advanced remarkably—we have powerful machine learning models, impressive AI demonstrations, and significant investments in AI by busi-nesses. Yet perplexingly, aggregate productivity growth in many economies has remained modest.

The likely explanation is the same dynamic seen with earlier GPTs. It takes time and substantial effort to retool businesses and workforce skills to fully exploit AI. New business processes, organizational structures, and worker training are the "co-inventions" needed to make AI truly productive. Until those catch up, the produc-tivity payoff will be limited.

This doesn't mean AI's impact won't happen; rather, history teaches us the opposite—with patience and proper complementary changes, the productivity boost will eventually arrive. Companies are currently building up "intangible as-sets" related to AI (data infrastructure, employee know-how, AI-ready processes) which don't immediately show up in economic statistics but set the stage for future growth.

The key insight for leaders is that simply having powerful AI technology is not enough to guarantee immediate gains. The technology must be accompanied by in-novation in how we organize work and production. This leads us to what business leaders should do to position their organizations for success in the AI era.

1.4 Capturing AI's GPT Potential: A Playbook for Leaders

Understanding AI as a general purpose technology helps leaders see that success-ful adoption goes far beyond installing new tools. The real gains come when orga-nizations rethink how they work, invest in people, and reshape their culture and operations to fit a new era.

Reimagining Business Processes

When electricity first entered factories, many simply swapped steam engines for electric motors without changing their layouts. The real transformation came only when they redesigned workflows to take full advantage of electricity's flexibility. The same is true for AI. Automating existing processes won't deliver big gains—rethinking them will.

Leaders should push their teams to redesign workflows around what AI makes possible. That might mean changing how customer service works, how products are developed, or how decisions are made. The greatest benefits come when organizations move from being **AI-enhanced** to becoming **AI-native** (Figure 1.4).

Complementary Investments for AI Success

Figure 1.4: Complementary Investments for AI Success. Key Insight for Leaders: AI Innovation requires investments in all layers of the pyramid, not just technology.

Investing in Skills and Human Capital

AI success depends on people, not just machines. Organizations need teams that can build AI systems, understand how to use them in context, and manage them effectively. That includes not just technical roles, but also domain experts, managers, and frontline workers.

This means broad investments in upskilling, internal training, external partnerships, and on-the-job learning. The same will hold true in the AI era.

Cultivating an AI-Friendly Organizational Culture

AI adoption requires a culture that encourages experimentation, embraces data-driven thinking, and supports continuous learning. Without that, even powerful tools may go unused, or worse, misused.

Leaders can shape this culture by setting a clear vision, encouraging collaboration between technical and business teams, and building trust in AI systems. When employees feel safe, valued, and engaged, they are more likely to explore and adopt new tools—and less likely to resist change.

Planning for Complementary Investments

AI doesn't work in a vacuum. It needs strong data, modern infrastructure, and new ways of working. That might mean investing in better IT systems, data quality, or tools tailored to the organization's needs.

These supporting investments are often invisible but essential. Just as a new forecasting model might require updates to supply chains or contracts, AI adoption often involves changes far beyond the tech team. Leaders should treat these as part of a unified strategy, not as separate initiatives.

Learning from Early Adopters While Avoiding Their Mistakes

Some organizations are already far along in their AI journeys, and there's much to learn from their successes. The best examples start with clear business goals, blend technical and domain expertise, and treat AI as a tool for augmentation, not just automation.

There are lessons in their missteps too—such as poor data quality, misaligned goals, or lack of user understanding. The smartest leaders don't just copy early adopters—they study what worked, what didn't, and why. That helps them move faster while avoiding common traps.

1.5 Conclusion: Preparing for the AI-Driven Future

Artificial intelligence marks a fundamental shift in capability, much like electricity or the steam engine in earlier eras. As a general purpose technology, AI is broad in application, improves steadily over time, and sparks innovation across the economy.

History shows that these kinds of technologies don't generate immediate productivity gains. Their impact depends on how organizations adapt—by redesigning processes, developing skills, and investing in complementary systems. That transformation takes time, but the long-term rewards are substantial.

As with electrification, the biggest gains will go to those who rethink how their organizations work—not just using AI to improve existing tasks, but to pursue new opportunities entirely. Simply adopting the tools won't be enough.

AI is not a passing trend. It's a foundational shift that will shape competitive advantage for decades. Those who recognize this and adapt their strategies, systems, and culture accordingly will be best positioned to lead in the years ahead.

2 Innovation Culture: Igniting AI Creativity in Organizations

Cheap experiments are worth more than good ideas.

—Michael Schrage

Innovation begins with experimentation. Organizations that excel at producing breakthrough ideas treat prototyping as a core practice, not just an occasional exercise. In this chapter, we'll explore how to foster a culture of AI innovation by emphasizing three key strategies: prototyping, experimentation, and engaging with lead users.

First, we'll discuss the importance of prototypes as *innovation catalysts*. Prototypes help teams turn abstract ideas into something tangible, sparking creative insights that discussions alone can't generate. We will see how rough prototypes often invite better feedback, setting the stage for rapid improvement.

Next, we'll explore how an *experimental mindset*—where hypotheses are tested through small, fast experiments—drives innovation. This shift from planning to action enables teams to learn quickly and adapt their approach based on real-world results, rather than relying on assumptions or over-analysis.

Finally, we'll cover how *engaging lead users*—those at the cutting edge of an industry—can accelerate innovation. These users push products to their limits and can reveal valuable insights that guide the next steps in development.

The ideas in this chapter are drawn from and adapted from the pioneering work of Michael Schrage (Schrage, 1999, 2014) and Eric von Hippel (von Hippel, 2005). Schrage's insights on innovation through prototyping and experimentation, alongside von Hippel's concept of "lead users," form the foundation of the strategies discussed here.

2.1 Prototypes as Innovation Catalysts

Prototypes help teams turn abstract ideas into concrete concepts. Even simple mockups reveal insights that discussions alone cannot. People don't order ingredients—they order meals. In other words, customers often can't describe what they want until they can see and interact with a prototype.

This is especially true with AI. A vague request for "more efficient operations" becomes clearer when a prototype—like a data visualization, a forecasting model, or a simulation—makes it tangible. A rough version provides something everyone can react to, clarify, and improve.

https://doi.org/10.1515/9783111583549-003

Interestingly, rough prototypes often generate better feedback than polished ones. When a model looks finished, people hesitate to criticize it. But a simple sketch or demo invites input and opens up creative possibilities, making it easier to imagine improvements.

The Shift from Planning to Playing

Companies that over-plan often overthink. Meetings multiply, and decision-makers become disconnected from customers and markets. Prototyping breaks this pattern by replacing analysis with action. Instead of endless debates, teams build something simple and test it in the real world.

This approach creates a low-cost, low-risk environment for experimentation, where the potential for learning is high.

Teams might produce several basic prototypes in a month, testing each with users. This turns innovation into a fast, high-yield process.

Collaborative Prototyping and Interdisciplinary Teams

Prototyping also fosters collaboration. When engineers, marketers, and operations teams gather around a model, their different perspectives spark unexpected insights. The prototype becomes a shared space—a conversation starter that breaks down silos and helps various disciplines find common ground. Collaborative prototyping is also a great way to build interdisciplinary teams, an essential requisite for AI success. These cross-functional experiences create shared understanding and vocabulary while establishing trust relationships that become invaluable when tackling complex AI challenges that inherently span multiple domains of expertise.

AI as a Prototyping Accelerator

AI tools make prototyping faster and more accessible than ever. Generative AI can create text, images, code, and simulations in days, reducing both the cost and complexity of experimentation.

Teams have found that using AI tools like large language models can cut the time to first prototype from months to weeks or days. A team working on an AI-driven service—such as a recommendation engine or a predictive maintenance system—can now build a demo in just a few days, test it with users, and quickly learn what works.

This speed also opens the door to people outside the technical core. No-code platforms and cloud services allow non-engineers to participate in serious experimentation. What once required a dedicated R&D team can now be done by small, cross-functional teams.

The key for leaders is to encourage this shift. Encourage experimentation. Invite teams to build small, rough models and learn from them. With today's tools, AI prototyping doesn't need to be expensive or complex—it just needs to happen often.

2.2 The Experimental Organization: Test and Learn

Prototypes turn ideas into things. Experiments turn things into insights. Instead of betting on big ideas, organizations should embrace a "test and learn" mindset. Rather than waiting for the perfect solution, organizations should run small experiments with prototypes and learn quickly.

From "Good Ideas" to Testable Hypotheses

One of the first steps in fostering an experimental mindset is moving away from vague "good ideas." Ideas, no matter how clever, don't have real value until they're testable. Innovation shifts from opinion to evidence when teams reframe creative suggestions as hypotheses.

For example, a vague proposal like "Let's improve customer service with AI" becomes more actionable when rephrased as, "If we use a chatbot to answer common questions, we expect to reduce call volume by 30 percent without lowering satisfaction." This clarity makes it easier to set up testing and measurement.

This approach is especially important for AI projects, where outcomes are often unpredictable. By treating AI initiatives as experiments, teams embrace learning. The key question shifts from "Did the project succeed?" to "What did we discover?"

From Low-Fidelity to High-Fidelity Prototypes

Rather than committing to a single, large-scale AI initiative, companies should experiment with many smaller prototypes. This allows organizations to test ideas at various levels of fidelity, starting with low-fidelity prototypes and working toward high-fidelity ones (Figure 2.1).
– **Low-fidelity prototypes** are rough, basic versions of a product or service—often made with minimal resources. These prototypes, such as wireframes, mock-ups, or paper sketches, allow teams to quickly test core concepts without

AI Prototype Development

Figure 2.1: **AI Prototype Development Spectrum.** This diagram illustrates the progression from low-fidelity to high-fidelity AI prototypes. As fidelity increases, so do time, cost, and risk—but also the quality of insights for product development.

investing significant time or money. They are ideal for gathering early feedback and identifying major issues before committing to a more developed version.

- **High-fidelity prototypes**, on the other hand, are more refined, often resembling the final product in terms of functionality and design. These prototypes are used for more detailed testing with users and can help validate the design, user experience, and functionality more thoroughly. The process of moving from low-fidelity to high-fidelity prototypes enables rapid iteration, allowing teams to refine their ideas and improve based on real-world testing.

Managing a Portfolio of Prototypes

Just as organizations manage a portfolio of projects, they can manage a portfolio of prototypes. This approach helps balance experimentation with strategic objectives. Instead of putting all resources into one prototype, companies can distribute their efforts across several prototypes, each serving a different purpose and testing different hypotheses.

One way to organize this portfolio is by using a 2×2 **matrix** (Figure 2.2) that classifies prototypes based on **risk** and **impact**:

- **Moderate Impact, Low Risk ("Quick Wins"):** These are tactical improvements that deliver significant value with established technologies and methods. They solve known problems with proven approaches, often enhancing existing systems or processes. Their impact is immediate and measurable, making them reliable investments with predictable outcomes.
- **High Impact, High Risk ("Game Changers"):** These are strategic innovations that potentially transform entire business models or create new market categories. They often involve emerging technologies, novel approaches, or fundamental paradigm shifts. Their impact isn't just large—it's potentially disruptive

Figure 2.2: AI Innovation Portfolio Matrix. This 2 × 2 matrix guides organizations in balancing their AI prototype investments across risk and impact dimensions. It helps prioritize resources between tactical "Quick Wins," transformative "Game Changers," capability-building "Skill Builders," and forward-looking "Strategic Learning" initiatives, with suggested allocation percentages varying based on organizational talent, risk appetite, industry context, and strategic priorities.

and can redefine what's possible. The higher risk comes from greater uncertainty, longer time horizons, and more complex implementation challenges.

- **Low Impact, Low Risk ("Skill Builders"):** These prototypes are simple to create and test, with minimal business impact. However, they serve an important purpose in building team capabilities, developing technical fluency, and fostering an innovation culture in a low-stakes environment. They help teams understand new tools or methodologies that enable more ambitious projects in the future.

- **Uncertain Impact, High Risk ("Strategic Learning"):** These prototypes explore unproven concepts with uncertain applications. They function as R&D investments that build organizational knowledge in emerging areas and may uncover unexpected innovation pathways. While their immediate business impact may be limited, these high-risk explorations could eventually lead to substantial payoffs. They represent short-term investments with uncertain but potentially high long-term returns, creating technological options and competitive insights that could become tomorrow's game changers.

Managing prototypes in this way ensures that teams are not just testing ideas at random but are strategically pursuing a diverse set of initiatives that balance potential reward with the likelihood of success.

The Value of Failure

In this experimental mindset, failure is not the opposite of success—it's part of the process. The goal of an experiment is not to immediately solve a problem, but to learn something valuable. Even if an experiment doesn't go as planned, the insights gained can help avoid much larger, more expensive mistakes down the road.

Quick experiments often provide more value at a fraction of the cost. A small test that disproves an assumption can be more valuable than a lengthy project with unclear results. When measured by the knowledge gained, these experiments deliver disproportionate returns.

Building a Fast, Frugal Testing Culture

A culture of experimentation doesn't emerge on its own. Leaders must actively encourage and reward quick, smart experiments—even when the results aren't positive. It's important to create an environment where experimenting, and even failing, is safe. As Jeff Bezos of Amazon puts it, "To invent, you have to experiment. And if you know in advance it's going to work, it's not an experiment" (Mancini, 2024).

This is especially critical in AI, where uncertainty is high. Teams need the freedom to try things that might not pan out, without fear of repercussions.

The Continuous Learning Loop

The true power of experimentation lies in its repetition. Teams form a hypothesis, run a test, analyze the data, and refine their approach. Over time, this process creates a loop of continuous improvement.

This shift also changes decision-making. Rather than relying on hierarchy or seniority, the focus moves to evidence. What matters is not who made the suggestion, but what the experiment reveals. This turns organizations into learning systems, where action is driven by data, not just authority.

Additionally, regular experimentation builds valuable skills within teams. As they run more tests, they become faster, smarter, and more creative. The company doesn't just get better results—it develops better people.

For leaders, the message is clear: encourage teams to test small ideas quickly, help them form hypotheses, support their learning, and celebrate the insights they generate, no matter the outcome.

2.3 Small Teams, Big Learning

The concepts from Michael Schrage's *Serious Play* (Schrage, 1999) and *The Innovator's Hypothesis* (Schrage, 2014) point to a simple but effective path forward. Organizations don't need a massive AI rollout to begin; they need small, talented teams, the freedom to experiment, and a focus on rapid learning.

Forming Small, Autonomous Teams

Start by forming several small, diverse teams—ideally five to seven people per team—bringing together a mix of technical and business experience. The teams should have the freedom to define both the business challenge and the prototype solution. Their task is not to create a business case but to build something—anything—that might help address the problem they identify.

Ask each team to prototype a simple solution, whether it's a dashboard, a chatbot, or a forecasting tool. Provide them with modest budgets and tight timelines. Stress that the goal is learning, not perfection. Constraints, combined with creative freedom, often produce the best results.

Creating a Culture of Psychological Safety and Fast Learning

Creating psychological safety within each team is essential. Team members need to know that failure won't hurt their reputation. When an experiment doesn't succeed, focus on what it taught rather than why it failed. Recognize and celebrate the most insightful experiments each quarter, even if they don't lead to a successful product. This sends a clear message: curiosity and learning matter more than being right.

To move quickly, teams need the right tools. Provide access to sample data, cloud-based AI tools, basic computing resources, and occasional technical support. They don't need a full-scale enterprise AI platform. What they need is a space where small, safe experiments can be run without bureaucratic delay.

Coaching teams to work in fast cycles is also critical. One useful approach is a four-week loop: identify a hypothesis, build a prototype, test it with users, then reflect and plan the next step. In just a month, teams can complete one or two full iterations and generate real learning. If something works, build on it. If not, move on. Either way, the organization moves forward.

Product Development as Scientific Experimentation

Product development should be treated as scientific experimentation. Each experiment builds on the knowledge and insights from previous experiments. Failures are as valuable—often more valuable—than successes, as they provide critical lessons. But for this to work, experiments must be documented and recorded. This ensures that insights are captured, learnings are shared, and teams can build on what's been tested, avoiding redundant efforts and accelerating progress.

The Role of Leadership: Fostering Cooperation and Competition

Leaders play an important role in fostering both cooperation and competitionindexcooperation and competition among teams. While each team defines its own business challenge and prototype, leaders can encourage collaboration by facilitating cross-team exchanges and sharing insights. At the same time, healthy competition can drive innovation by challenging teams to produce the best solutions quickly. Regular check-ins—such as a brief conversation—help keep things aligned and remove obstacles. Leaders should ask, "What did you do? What did you learn? What's next?" These updates allow leaders to spot promising ideas to scale and invest in them when the time is right.

As more teams experiment, others will follow. The early pilots will serve as models for the rest of the organization. Over time, the company's approach to AI adoption will shift from technology procurement to hands-on discovery. People will learn AI by using it, and the organization will build its internal capacity through building, testing, and learning.

2.4 Engaging Lead Users: Innovation from the Outside In

While internal teams are essential for innovation, some of the best ideas come from outside the company—from the customers and users who are already pushing your products to their limits. These users, often called "lead users," face needs that the broader market hasn't yet experienced. In attempting to solve these needs, they often invent the future (Figure 2.3).

Identifying Lead Users

Lead users are the tinkerers, hackers, and early adopters who stretch products beyond their original design. They build workarounds, request features you haven't thought of, and offer insights into what the broader market will want tomorrow.

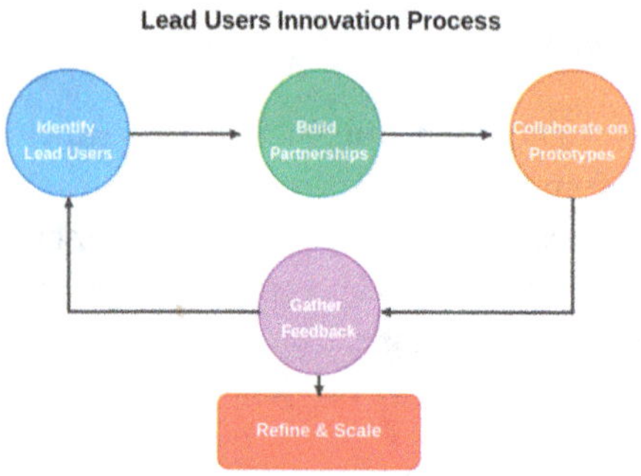

Lead Users Innovation Process

Figure 2.3: Lead Users Innovation Process. This diagram illustrates the cyclical nature of innovation through lead user engagement. The process begins with identifying lead users who push products to their limits, followed by building partnerships with these users. Next, organizations collaborate on prototype development, gather feedback through continuous testing, and finally refine and scale successful solutions. This approach creates a perpetual learning loop that drives innovation from the outside in.

These users often solve their own problems, usually without expecting recognition or reward.

Examples of lead users can be found in many industries. Surgeons modify tools to meet complex medical needs. Power users script custom software solutions. Logistics teams adapt systems for extreme conditions. These are the users who innovate at the edges, showing you where the real value lies.

To tap into this valuable source of innovation, start by identifying these advanced users. Look for customers who use your products in unusual ways, request advanced features, or work in challenging environments. You can find them through support tickets, user forums, or by asking frontline employees who your most inventive customers are.

Distinguishing Lead Users from Vocal Customers

It's important to note that the lead user approach differs fundamentally from broad customer feedback initiatives or responding to vocal customers with niche feature requests. Lead users aren't merely those who speak the loudest or demand customizations that serve only their specific needs. Rather, they represent the leading edge of market trends and uncover nascent needs that will become mainstream in the future. While general customer feedback captures current desires of the average user, lead users illuminate emerging possibilities not yet articulated by the broader market. The lead user methodology involves systematically identifying these pioneering users and collaboratively developing innovations that solve emerging problems, ultimately creating breakthrough products with broad market potential—not isolated features serving narrow interests.

Building Partnerships with Lead Users

Once you've identified your lead users, it's time to bring them in. Invite them to collaborate with your teams by hosting workshops, offering early access to experimental features, and setting up regular feedback sessions. The goal is to form a partnership: they get the tools that meet their needs, and you gain valuable insights into where the market is heading.

This collaboration benefits both sides. Lead users help refine your products and often reveal unmet needs that can shape the future of your offerings. At the same time, they gain access to solutions that better meet their demands, strengthening their relationship with your brand.

Case Studies

Many companies have successfully used this strategy. For example, 3M worked with hospital technicians to develop surgical tape that addressed real-world demands, resulting in a more successful product (von Hippel et al., 1999). Similarly, Lego collaborated with adult hobbyists to improve its robotics kits, leading to stronger, more innovative products (Antorini et al., 2012; Hienerth et al., 2014).

With AI, lead users might already be experimenting on their own—building small models, automating parts of their workflow, or developing predictive tools. By engaging with these users, organizations can accelerate innovation by sharing prototypes and building solutions together. Their feedback can help companies refine AI products, ensuring they meet the needs of both early adopters and the broader market.

Creating Feedback Loops for Continuous Innovation

One of the key advantages of working with lead users is the ability to establish feedback loops. A lead user identifies a need, your team develops a rough solution, and the lead user tests it. This continuous exchange can uncover valuable opportunities much faster than any internal roadmap.

These feedback loops accelerate product development by ensuring that the solutions you build are aligned with real, on-the-ground needs. Lead users provide insights that might not be apparent from internal research, making them invaluable collaborators in the innovation process.

2.5 Conclusion

In this chapter, we've explored how organizations can foster a culture of innovation by focusing on prototypes, experimentation, and collaboration with lead users. We began by discussing the importance of prototyping as a catalyst for innovation, emphasizing the role of low-fidelity to high-fidelity prototypes in generating insights and learning.

Next, we highlighted the shift from traditional planning to a "test and learn" mindset, where experiments—both small and large—provide valuable knowledge that drives progress. The concept of managing a portfolio of prototypes was introduced, ensuring that teams balance risk and impact as they experiment and iterate.

We then explored the importance of building a culture that treats product development as scientific experimentation, where failures are just as valuable as successes. Documenting and sharing these experiments ensures that valuable lessons are passed along, building a collective knowledge base that drives continuous improvement.

Finally, we examined how engaging lead users—those who push products to their limits—can unlock powerful innovations. By building partnerships with these users, organizations can gain critical insights into market needs, accelerate product development, and create solutions that meet the future demands of the market.

Taken together, these strategies provide a pragmatic approach to innovation that encourages collaboration, continuous learning, and the shared pursuit of improvement.

Part II: **Computation**

3 Algorithms: The Logic of Computing

> Without algorithms, computers would be useless, and none of modern technology would exist.
>
> —Panos Louridas

Algorithms provide the logic that drives all computing, including artificial intelligence. In this chapter, we explore what algorithms are, how they work, and why they serve as the backbone of AI systems.

We begin with everyday examples to build an intuitive understanding. Then, we walk through a simple algorithm to highlight its key components. Finally, we introduce the idea of algorithmic efficiency—how the same task can be performed not just correctly, but faster and more effectively. This matters immensely for AI, where systems must process vast amounts of data and perform billions of operations in fractions of a second.

3.1 What Is an Algorithm?

Let's begin with an informal definition:

Definition. An algorithm is a precise series of instructions for transforming input data into an output.

This simple definition highlights three essential elements. First, an algorithm consists of step-by-step *instructions*, each clearly specifying what to do. Second, it requires *input* data. Third, by following each instruction, it produces a meaningful result, called *output* (Figure 3.1).

input ·········◄—— series of instructions ——►········ ·output

Figure 3.1: The Three Core Elements of an Algorithm: Instructions, Input, and Output. The rectangular box represents the series of instructions that transforms the input (left arrow) into the output (right arrow).

To make this idea more tangible, consider a familiar example: making a peanut butter sandwich, as shown in Algorithm 1.

Even this simple algorithm illustrates a key challenge: natural language is often vague. How much peanut butter should one use? What does "spread evenly" mean? Although humans tolerate ambiguity, computers do not. Algorithms require pre-

https://doi.org/10.1515/9783111583549-005

Algorithm 1 How to Make a Peanut Butter Sandwich.

Gather the following ingredients and tools: sliced bread, peanut butter, knife, and a plate.
Place one slice of bread on the plate.
Use the knife to spread peanut butter evenly on the slice of bread.
Place a second slice of bread on top of the peanut butter.
Serve the sandwich!

---

cision; each instruction must have exactly one interpretation to ensure consistent results.

Despite these details, all algorithms share the same basic structure: inputs, a sequence of clearly defined steps that operate on the input, and an output.

Loops and Branches

Two key concepts dramatically expand the power of algorithms: **loops** (repeating steps) and **branching** (making choices). We can illustrate both by extending our sandwich algorithm to handle multiple orders—and adding the option for jelly, as shown in Algorithm 2.

Algorithm 2 Making Multiple Sandwiches with Options.

1: **Input:** A list of sandwich orders, each marked as PB (peanut butter only) or PBJ (peanut butter and jelly)
2: Gather ingredients: bread, peanut butter, jelly, and plates
3: **while** orders remain in list **do**
4:      Place bread slice on a clean plate
5:      Spread peanut butter on the bread
6:      **if** current order is marked PBJ **then**
7:          Add jelly on top of peanut butter
8:      **end if**
9:      Top with second bread slice
10:     Remove current order from list
11: **end while**
12: **Output:** One sandwich prepared for each order in the input list

---

The while statement in Algorithm 2 creates a loop: a cycle of repeated steps that continues until all sandwich orders are fulfilled. Like a chef during a lunch rush, the algorithm prepares each sandwich by repeating the same instructions for

Figure 3.2: The while Loop. This diagram illustrates how a while loop works in programming. The top box shows a program's normal sequential flow of instructions. The middle box represents a loop structure, where a set of instructions repeats multiple times based on a condition. Only when the condition is no longer true does the program continue to the bottom box, resuming the sequential execution pattern.

every order in the list (Figure 3.2). (A for loop is another common way to express repetition.)

The if statement in Algorithm 2 creates a decision point where the algorithm chooses between two paths—adding jelly or proceeding directly to the next step. This ability to make conditional choices allows a single algorithm to adapt to different scenarios without needing separate instructions for each variation (Figure 3.3).

Together, loops and branching transform simple instructions into sophisticated problem-solving tools. Loops efficiently handle repetitive tasks, while branching provides a mechanism to handle variable pathways. These fundamental constructs are the building blocks that give algorithms their remarkable flexibility and power.

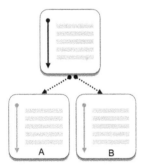

Figure 3.3: The Branching Decision. This diagram demonstrates how an if statement creates a decision point in a program. After following the sequential instructions in the top box, the program encounters a decision (the if statement). Based on whether a specific condition is true or false, the program will follow only one path—either executing the instructions in Box A or Box B—before continuing with the rest of the program.

3.2 An Algorithm in Action

Let's bridge the gap between everyday tasks and computer code by examining a simple algorithm written in Python. Like the sandwich example, the program expressed in Algorithm 3 follows a clear sequence of steps—this time, to calculate the average of a list of numbers.

Algorithm 3 Python Program to Calculate Mean.

```
1:  numbers = [4, 7, 1, 3, 9, 2, 5]
2:  sum = 0
3:  for num in numbers do
4:      sum += num
5:  end for
6:  mean = sum / len(numbers)
7:  print(f"The mean is: {mean}")
```

Unlike the sandwich example—which allows room for interpretation (what does "spread evenly" mean?)—computer algorithms must be completely unambiguous. Every instruction must have a single, precise meaning. For example, the word average might mean different things in everyday language (mean, median, or mode), but in this program, it clearly refers to the mean. This kind of precision is what makes algorithms dependable tools for solving problems.

Step-by-Step: The Mean Calculation in Action

Input: A list of seven numbers: 4, 7, 1, 3, 9, 2, and 5.
1. **Initialize a variable** called sum to zero. This will keep track of the running total.
2. **Iterate through the list** and add each number to sum. Here's how it changes:
   - $4 \rightarrow$ sum = 4
   - $7 \rightarrow$ sum = 11
   - $1 \rightarrow$ sum = 12
   - $3 \rightarrow$ sum = 15
   - $9 \rightarrow$ sum = 24
   - $2 \rightarrow$ sum = 26
   - $5 \rightarrow$ sum = 31
3. **Compute the mean** by dividing the total by the number of values:
   mean = 31 / 7 $\approx$ 4.43
Output: "The mean of our numbers is 4.43"

This straightforward algorithm demonstrates three foundational principles that appear in virtually all computational systems:

First, it processes a collection of data items one at a time using a loop, a fundamental technique for handling data efficiently, whether we are dealing with a handful of values or millions. Second, it maintains state by keeping track of a running total across iterations: this "memory" between steps is essential in nearly all algorithms. Third, it applies multiple transformations to the data to produce a result or output.

These same principles are at the heart of more advanced systems, including artificial intelligence. Whether evaluating patterns in data, optimizing decisions, or generating predictions, AI models still rely on the same core pattern.

While modern algorithms may operate on a massive scale and involve sophisticated techniques, their underlying logic remains consistent. Whether calculating an average, guiding a robot, or powering intelligent systems, algorithms thrive on this simple yet powerful structure: clear, step-by-step instructions that turn data into meaningful outputs.

3.3 Making Algorithms Better

As we've seen, algorithms provide the structure for solving problems. But not all algorithms are created equal. Skilled programmers don't just look for a solution—they look for the best one. This focus on quality and performance is what turns a functional algorithm into an exceptional one.

The Quest for Efficiency

When evaluating a problem, computer scientists typically ask three questions:
- Is there an algorithm that can solve it?
- How long does the algorithm take to run?
- Can it be done faster?

This mindset emphasizes not just solving a problem, but solving it efficiently.

In some situations, speed differences may seem trivial: whether a smart phone takes 0.001 or 0.0001 seconds to calculate a tip hardly matters. But in AI systems that process billions of data points, those differences can mean the difference between seconds and days.

A Tale of Two Search Methods

To see why efficiency matters, consider a simple number guessing game. Someone has picked a number between 1 and 1,000—say, 777. After each guess, you're told whether the target is higher or lower than your guess.

Standard Search: One by One

The most straightforward method is to check each number in order: 1, 2, 3, and so on. To reach 777, you'd need 777 guesses. This works, but it's painfully slow as the range increases.

Binary Search: Divide and Conquer

A more efficient strategy is to halve the search space with each guess. This is called binary search. Here's how binary search would find 777 in a range from 1 to 1,000:

Binary Search in Action: Finding 777

- Guess 500 → "Higher"
- Guess 750 → "Higher"
- Guess 875 → "Lower"
- Guess 812 → "Lower"
- Guess 781 → "Lower"
- Guess 765 → "Higher"
- Guess 773 → "Higher"
- Guess 777 → "Found it"

Just 8 guesses instead of 777. Even in the worst case (guessing 1,000) binary search would take only 10 steps. Each guess cuts the possible range in half, reducing the number of steps needed to find the answer.

The contrast is striking:
- Standard search: 777 guesses.
- Binary search: 8 guesses.

Why Efficiency Matters at Scale

The power of efficient algorithms becomes clear at large scale. Imagine searching for a specific entry in a database containing one billion records:
- A standard search might require up to **750 million** steps.
- A binary search would need only **30** steps.

That's the difference between minutes—or even hours—and a fraction of a second. It's a striking example of how algorithm choice can have immense consequences at scale.

The Impact on AI Systems

In AI, efficiency isn't optional—it's essential. Modern AI systems handle vast datasets and perform complex computations that would be impossible without optimized algorithms.

For example, training a neural network to recognize images may involve analyzing millions of pictures and adjusting billions of internal parameters on each pass. Without efficient algorithms, that process could take years instead of hours or minutes.

Some of the most significant breakthroughs in AI have come not just from more data or faster hardware, but from **smarter algorithms**. These innovations allow AI systems to tackle increasingly complex problems while remaining fast enough for real-time use.

3.4 Algorithmic Speed

Imagine two chefs making the same chocolate cake. One takes 30 minutes, the other takes 2 hours. For hungry cake lovers, that difference matters! Similarly, two algorithms might solve the same problem, but one does it much faster, especially as the size of the data grows.

The Speed Test: Introducing Big O Notation

To compare algorithm performance, computer scientists use a convention called *Big O notation*. It does not measure exact speed; it describes how the running time of an algorithm increases as the input size increases. It's like asking: *If I double the data, how long will this take?*

Here are a few common types:
- $O(1)$—Constant time: speed stays the same, no matter the input size.
- $O(\log n)$—Logarithmic time: each step cuts the problem in half.
- $O(n)$—Linear time: time grows directly with the input size.
- $O(n^2)$—Quadratic time: time increases rapidly as data grows.

Why It Matters

Even small differences in efficiency can have a huge impact at scale. For example, when searching through one billion items:
- An $O(n)$ algorithm might take several minutes.
- An $O(\log n)$ algorithm could finish in just 30 steps.

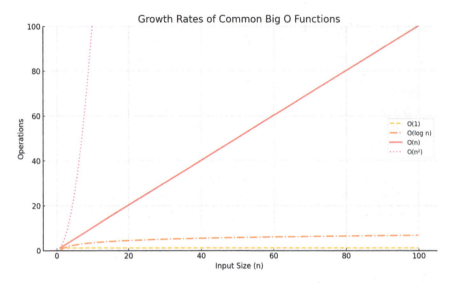

Figure 3.4: Growth Rates of Common Big O functions. $O(1)$ remains constant regardless of input size. $O(\log n)$ and $O(n)$ grow gradually, while $O(n^2)$ accelerates quickly—showing how inefficient algorithms can become impractical at scale.

In AI systems, where datasets are massive, choosing the right algorithm can be the difference between real-time performance and unacceptable delays. Figure 3.4 displays the growth rates of Common Big O functions.

Understanding algorithm speed helps us write better code, build smarter systems, and create tools that stay responsive—no matter how big the problem gets.

Conclusion

At its core, an algorithm is a clear, step-by-step recipe for solving a problem. Whether it's calculating an average or powering a recommendation system, the same basic principles apply: process the data, keep track of what matters, and transform inputs into meaningful results.

We've seen how some algorithms are faster than others—and why that speed is crucial. With Big O notation, we can evaluate algorithms not just by whether they work, but by how well they scale as data grows. An efficient algorithm can mean the difference between a problem that's solvable and one that's hopelessly out of reach.

The most powerful systems in today's world—from search engines to AI—are built on simple ideas, executed well. That's the beauty of algorithms: small, thoughtful steps can lead to a big impact.

4 Architecture: How Computers Work

> People who are more than casually interested in computers should have at least some idea of what the underlying hardware is like. Otherwise the programs they write will be pretty weird.
>
> —Donald Knuth

What exactly is a computer, and how does it work? In this chapter, we look under the hood to understand the architecture that makes computation possible. We begin with the EDVAC, the first general-purpose digital computer, and the design that became the blueprint for nearly all modern machines: *the von Neumann architecture*. From there, we examine its core components, walk through a simple program in action, and trace how the architecture evolved into multi-core processors and specialized hardware like GPUs, which now power AI and modern computing at scale.

4.1 Inventing the Modern Computer

In the early 20th century, a "computer" referred not to a machine, but to a person who performed calculations by hand. That changed dramatically with the development of *electronic computing machines* during World War II. One of the first, the ENIAC (Electronic Numerical Integrator and Computer), was completed in 1945 by a team led by John Mauchly and J. Presper Eckert at the University of Pennsylvania. Designed to compute artillery firing tables for the U.S. Army, it soon found a new role verifying calculations for nuclear weapons research (Denning and Martell, 2015).

As the team began work on a successor machine—the EDVAC (Electronic Discrete Variable Automatic Computer)—two members of the ENIAC project, Arthur Burks and Herman Goldstine, invited mathematician John von Neumann to join the effort. While much of the architectural groundwork came from Eckert and Mauchly, von Neumann played a pivotal role in formalizing and articulating the design (Figure 4.1). His 1945 document, *First Draft of a Report on the EDVAC*, captured the essential features of the new architecture and became the most widely circulated account, helping to shape the conceptual foundation of modern computing (von Neumann, 2021).

This framework, now called the **von Neumann architecture**, laid the foundation for nearly all modern computers. It introduced a simple but powerful idea: a general-purpose machine could carry out any computation by following instructions stored in memory, rather than being physically rewired for each new task. By organizing the computer around a small set of well-defined components that handled both data and instructions in a unified way, the design achieved remarkable

https://doi.org/10.1515/9783111583549-006

Figure 4.1: John von Neumann. One of the foremost mathematicians of the 20th century and a true polymath. His contributions spanned mathematics, physics, computer science, and economics. The architecture that bears his name laid the foundation for modern computing devices.

clarity and flexibility. Created under tight constraints—unreliable components, limited memory, and high cost—it remains a striking example of functional elegance: a system that achieves power through simplicity.

Von Neumann's report began with a clear ambition:

> "The considerations which follow deal with the structure of a *very high speed automatic digital computing system*, and in particular with its *logical control*."

At its core, a computing machine executes algorithms—step-by-step instructions for solving a task. What made von Neumann's model revolutionary was how it organized this task. It introduced three defining principles into modern computing:

- **Binary Representation:** Unlike the decimal-based ENIAC, the EDVAC used binary—representing all numbers and instructions as sequences of 0s and 1s. This shift simplified the underlying electronics, particularly with components like vacuum tubes that could be more easily configured to represent two states (on and off). Binary encoding not only made arithmetic and logical operations more straightforward, it also laid the groundwork for taking advantage of digital circuits, which would later become central to modern computing.
- **Stored Program:** Instead of hardwiring instructions into the machine, as with ENIAC, EDVAC treated the program itself as input. Instructions could be encoded as data, stored in memory, and executed step by step. This conceptual breakthrough separated the logic of a computation from the hardware that carried it out, laying the foundation for modern software.
  (**Note:** The idea had been anticipated as early as 1843 by Charles Babbage and Ada Lovelace in their design of the Analytical Engine, but it took another century to be realized in practice.)

- **Unified Memory:** EDVAC used a single memory system to hold both data and program instructions. While not essential to the stored-program concept, this design choice simplified hardware construction and allowed for more efficient use of limited memory resources—an important consideration when components were expensive and fragile.

Together, these principles defined a machine that could perform virtually any computation. This was the breakthrough: a general-purpose, programmable, digital computer. The von Neumann architecture became the template for hardware in the computing age.

4.2 The Core Components of a von Neumann Machine

Let's now examine the core components of a von Neumann machine. A computer is a machine that executes a sequence of instructions—called a program—to transform input into output. Each instruction tells the machine to carry out a specific operation, such as adding two numbers, comparing values, or moving data from one location to another. These operations are deliberately simple, designed to be performed quickly and reliably by hardware. A key innovation was the realization that even complex calculations, like solving a nonlinear differential equation, could be broken down into a sequence of such elementary steps.

The von Neumann architecture organizes a computer into four principal components that work together to perform computation (see Figure 4.2):

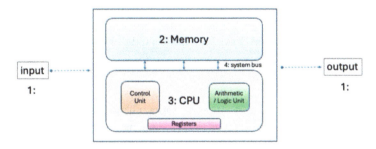

Figure 4.2: Von Neumann Architecture: Diagram illustrating the four key components—(1) Input/Output Devices, (2) Memory, and (3) CPU, which contains the Control Unit and Arithmetic Logic Unit (ALU). Modern computers often include internal features such as registers and a system bus (depicted here), which facilitate communication and temporary storage within the CPU.

1. **Arithmetic/Logic Unit (ALU):** The ALU performs simple mathematical operations (like addition and subtraction) and logical comparisons. Von Neumann originally called this component the *Central Arithmetic* (CA) unit. It is the computer's core calculator.
2. **Control Unit:** This component sequences and manages the execution of instructions. It fetches instructions from memory, interprets them, and coordinates other components to carry out each step. Von Neumann referred to it as the *Central Control* (CC) unit. Together with the ALU, it forms the Central Processing Unit (CPU).
3. **Memory:** Memory stores both the program (instructions) and the data it operates on. Think of memory as a large set of numbered boxes, each capable of holding a value. The computer reads from and writes to these boxes using their address.
4. **Input/Output Devices:** These devices connect the computer to the outside world. Input devices (like keyboards or sensors) feed data into the system; output devices (like displays or printers) present results. They translate between human-understandable forms and the binary language of machines.

Von Neumann vs. Turing Machine

The von Neumann architecture and the Turing machine are both foundational models of computation, but they serve different purposes:
–   **Turing Machine:** A theoretical model introduced by Alan Turing in the 1930s to define what it means for a function to be computable. It consists of an infinite tape, a read/write head, and a finite set of rules.
–   **Von Neumann Architecture:** A practical model for building real computers. It defines how physical systems use memory, processing units, and control flow to execute stored programs.

Key difference: The Turing machine is a mathematical abstraction. The von Neumann architecture is an engineering blueprint. The two models are complementary; one tells us what is computable, the other how we compute in practice.

This elegant division of labor—computation, control, storage, and communication—demonstrates the enduring power of the von Neumann model. It is a modular, general-purpose design capable of executing any program that can be expressed as a sequence of instructions.

4.3 A Simple Programming Example

To see the von Neumann architecture in action, let's walk through a simple program. Our example performs the following steps:
1. Add two numbers.
2. Compare the result to a third number.
3. `Print 1` if they are equal; otherwise, `Print 0`.

We assume that both the program and its input data have already been loaded into memory:
- Address 100 holds the number 7.
- Address 101 holds the number 4.
- Address 102 holds the number 11.

Here is a simplified version of the program in pseudocode:

1: **LOAD** value at address 100
2: **ADD** value at address 101
3: **STORE** result at address 200
4: **LOAD** value at address 200
5: **COMPARE** to value at address 102
6: **PRINT** result of comparison

Each instruction is executed step by step by the components of the von Neumann architecture:
1. **Arithmetic Operation (Steps 1–2):** The processor fetches the first instruction: **LOAD** the value at address 100 (which is 7). This value is placed into a temporary register. The next instruction, **ADD**, retrieves the value at address 101 (which is 4) and adds it to the loaded value. The result (11) is held temporarily.
2. **Storing the Result (Step 3):** The **STORE** instruction writes the result (11) to memory at address 200.
3. **Comparison Operation (Steps 4–5):** The processor **LOAD**s the value at address 200 and compares it to the value at address 102 (also 11). The **COMPARE** instruction checks for equality and stores the result internally.
4. **Output (Step 6):** The **PRINT** instruction sends the comparison result to an output device, such as a screen or printer. In this case, the output would be 1, indicating the values are equal.

> **Claude Shannon: Turning Logic into Hardware**
>
> In 1937, Claude Shannon, then a graduate student at MIT, published a groundbreaking thesis showing how Boolean logic could be implemented using electrical switches. His insight connected two worlds:
> - **Boolean Algebra:** A formal system developed by George Boole in the 19th century to express logic using operations like AND, OR, and NOT.
> - **Electrical Circuits:** Practical arrangements of relays and switches used in telephone networks and early computing machines.
>
> Shannon demonstrated that logical operations could be performed mechanically using electrical circuits—a discovery that laid the foundation for digital computing. His work made it possible to design hardware that could carry out logical decisions automatically, turning binary logic from a mathematical concept into a physical reality. This breakthrough made computers like the EDVAC possible.

This simple example shows how a computer carries out a sequence of instructions, moving data between memory and processor to perform operations. Though each step is simple, the ability to chain them together gives computers the power to perform complex tasks—from basic arithmetic and file storage to graphics rendering and AI.

4.4 Multiple Cores

Modern processors often contain more than one execution unit, or **core**. Each core functions like an independent mini-CPU—with its own Control Unit and Arithmetic Logic Unit (ALU)—capable of running its own instruction stream (Figure 4.3).

In a single-core system, the processor can handle only one stream of instructions at a time. In contrast, a multicore processor can execute multiple streams in parallel, allowing the computer to perform different tasks at the same time. One core might handle user input, while another processes a spreadsheet or renders video.

Although each core operates independently, they all share access to the same system memory. This shared access can become a bottleneck when multiple cores try to read or write at once, since only one can access a memory location at a time. Effective coordination becomes essential, and not all tasks can be easily divided into parts that run in parallel.

Still, multi-core designs have transformed everyday computing. They allow modern systems to multitask more fluidly—streaming video, syncing files, and running applications simultaneously. Multicore processors are also critical in fields like data analysis, gaming, and real-time systems where responsiveness and concurrency matter.

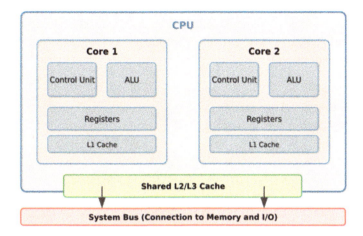

Figure 4.3: Multi-Core Processor Architecture. Each core includes its own Control Unit and Arithmetic Logic Unit (ALU), and can operate independently while sharing access to system memory and cache.

However, even multicore systems face limits, especially when problems require massive amounts of repetitive computation. That's where another kind of processor excels: the GPU, which we turn to next.

4.5 Graphics Processing Units

While CPUs were designed for general-purpose computing, many modern applications—especially in artificial intelligence—require massive amounts of parallel, data-intensive computation. That's where Graphics Processing Units (GPUs) come in.

From Graphics to AI

GPUs were originally developed to accelerate the rendering of images and video in games, a process that involves applying the same mathematical operations to large grids of pixels or vertices. These tasks are often written as nested loops—repeating the same computation over rows and columns—but they can be expressed more efficiently as **matrix operations**, which allow entire grids of values to be transformed in a single step. Such operations are ideal for parallel execution.

Unlike CPUs, which typically contain a handful of powerful cores optimized for sequential logic and branching, GPUs are built with thousands of simpler cores designed to execute the same operation on many data points simultaneously using matrix operations. This architecture makes them exceptionally well-suited to the kinds of repetitive, large-scale computation found in modern AI tasks—especially those involving matrix multiplication and other linear algebra operations central to neural networks (Figure 4.4).

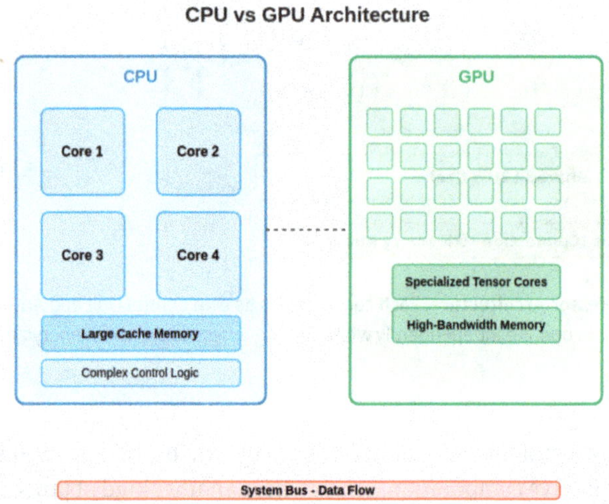

CPU vs GPU Architecture

Figure 4.4: Comparison of CPU and GPU architectures. CPUs feature a small number of complex cores optimized for diverse tasks. GPUs contain thousands of simpler cores specialized for parallel workloads. Modern GPUs also include high-bandwidth memory and specialized units like tensor cores for accelerating machine learning.

Parallel Power

If a CPU is like a skilled craftsman carefully completing one task at a time, a GPU is like a workshop filled with thousands of workers, each performing the same task on different pieces of material. For workloads such as training a neural network, where millions of simple operations must be repeated across large datasets, this massive parallelism delivers dramatic speedups.

In fact, many breakthroughs in deep learning over the past decade were made possible not just by more data or better algorithms, but by advances in GPU hardware.

CPUs and GPUs Together

Most AI systems combine CPUs and GPUs. The CPU handles overall program logic, coordination, and communication with storage and input/output devices. The GPU takes over for data-heavy computations, such as matrix multiplication and tensor operations.

This division of labor allows systems to remain flexible while accelerating the most demanding parts of computation. It's the combination—fast control and massive parallelism—that gives modern AI its power.

4.6 Conclusion

We began this chapter by asking a simple question: What makes a computer work? We traced the answer back to the 1940s, when the EDVAC team introduced a design that remains the blueprint for nearly all modern machines. The von Neumann architecture—based on a small set of well-defined components and a brilliant concept of storing instructions in memory—enabled computers to be reprogrammable, flexible, and powerful.

Over time, that elegant design has evolved. Modern systems still follow the basic structure, but they now include multiple processing cores and specialized hardware like GPUs to handle enormous workloads. These innovations haven't replaced the von Neumann model—they've extended it to meet the growing complexity and scale of modern computation.

Part III: **Machine Learning**

5 Machine Learning: Learning from Data

The field of machine learning is concerned with the question of how to construct computer programs that automatically improve with experience.

—Tom Mitchell

Ask a young child to pick out cats from a pile of pictures. They'll do it quickly and effortlessly. Ask the world's best programmers to write an algorithm that can do the same. They'll find it nearly impossible.

Why? As we saw in Chapter 3, traditional programming relies on precise, step-by-step instructions—what we called an algorithm. But what exactly defines a cat? Pointy ears? Whiskers? Fur patterns? Four legs? Cats can appear in endless poses, lighting conditions, and angles. They might be partly hidden, curled up, or stretched out. They could be indoors, outdoors, or somewhere in between. They might be next to people, furniture, or other animals. Writing instructions to cover every possibility is an insurmountable challenge.

In 1959, Arthur Samuel, a pioneer in artificial intelligence, defined machine learning as "the field of study that gives computers the ability to learn without being explicitly programmed" (Samuel, 1959). What if, instead of writing instructions, we gave a computer thousands—or millions—of cat photos and let it figure out the algorithm for identifying cats on its own? That's the basic idea behind machine learning.

This chapter explores how machine learning differs from traditional programming—and why that difference matters. We'll begin by comparing the two approaches to show what makes machine learning so powerful. Then we'll look at a breakthrough moment in the field—the ImageNet challenge—which showed how far machine learning has come, even outperforming humans in some tasks. Finally, we'll explore the main types of machine learning: *supervised*, *unsupervised*, and *reinforcement*. We'll focus on supervised learning because it's central to how machines learn to make predictions.

5.1 Traditional Programming vs. Machine Learning

Computers traditionally follow precise instructions created by humans. These step-by-step procedures, called algorithms, work like recipes: specific inputs, clear steps, predictable outputs. Consider mortgage calculations. A programmer codes an exact formula using loan amount, interest rate, and term to determine monthly payments. This approach excels when rules are clear and consistent. It powers banking systems, word processors, smartphone applications, and countless other tools we use daily.

https://doi.org/10.1515/9783111583549-008

But not all problems can be solved with a traditional approach. Some tasks are too complex. Take credit card fraud detection. The patterns are intricate, with countless subtle indicators that might signal suspicious activity. Understanding spoken language presents similar complexity. People speak with different accents, vocabulary, sentence structures, and dialects. Even predicting which customers might cancel a subscription—a problem known as churn prediction—depends on countless interrelated and subtle factors that resist simple rule-based analysis.

In these cases, traditional programming falls short. The rules are too numerous or too intricate to express as code.

Machine Learning vs. Traditional Programming

Machine learning fundamentally inverts the traditional programming approach. As illustrated in Figure 5.1, traditional programming requires humans to explicitly write the rules (the program), which together with data are provided as inputs to the computer to produce the desired output.

Traditional Programming Paradigm

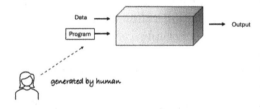

Figure 5.1: Traditional Programming Paradigm. In this approach, a human programmer provides both the program and the data as inputs to the computer, which then produces the desired output. In Chapter 3, we saw the example of a program written by humans to calculate the mean of a set of numbers.

In contrast, Figure 5.2 shows how machine learning transforms this process. Instead of manually coding the rules, we let the computer discover them by studying examples. We provide historical data paired with the expected outputs, and the AI system automatically generates the program by finding patterns in this data. Once created, this program, as before, can then be used like traditional software to process new data and produce outputs.

The critical difference lies in how the rules are created: in traditional programming, humans define the rules based on their understanding of the problem; in ma-

Machine Learning Paradigm

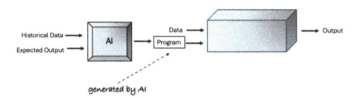

Figure 5.2: The Machine Learning Paradigm. Instead of writing a program by hand, a model is first trained on data and expected outputs. The program, in the form of a 'learned model', is generated by AI and then applied to new data to generate predictions.

chine learning, the system learns the rules directly from the data. This shift allows computers to tackle problems where the patterns are too complex, subtle, or varied for humans to program by hand (Table 5.1).

Table 5.1: Some key differences between traditional programming and machine learning.

Traditional Programming	Machine Learning
Algorithms written by humans	Algorithms learned from data
Rules are explicitly coded	Rules are inferred from examples
Changes require manual updates	Models are retrained with new data
Best for stable, well-defined tasks	Best for complex, data-rich problems

Spam filtering illustrates this well. Instead of relying on programmers to define every possible spam rule, machine learning systems analyze thousands of labeled emails—"spam" or "not spam"—and learn the patterns themselves. Many of these patterns are subtle or unexpected, often beyond what a human would think to encode.

The strength of machine learning lies in its ability to uncover complex patterns that are hard to describe explicitly. As more data becomes available, the model can be retrained to improve its performance—no code rewrites needed, though additional training is still required to incorporate new examples.

To see just how powerful this approach can be, we now turn to a key moment in the history of machine learning—the ImageNet breakthrough. It marked a turning point, when computers began to outperform humans in image recognition, a task once thought far beyond their reach.

5.2 The ImageNet Breakthrough

A pivotal moment in machine learning came in 2012 with the ImageNet breakthrough, which transformed the field of image recognition.

ImageNet is a massive dataset of over 14 million labeled images, grouped into thousands of categories. Before 2012, image classification systems struggled, misclassifying about 25–30 % of images. That changed when Geoffrey Hinton and his team at the University of Toronto introduced *AlexNet*, a deep learning model that slashed the error rate to 16.4 %—a remarkable improvement (Krizhevsky et al., 2012).

ImageNet Challenge Timeline

- **2006**—AI scientist Fei-Fei Li starts the ImageNet project.
- **2010**—The annual ImageNet Large Scale Visual Recognition Challenge (ILSVRC) is launched. The first ILSVRC achieves a 28.2 % error rate.
- **2012**—A deep convolutional neural network called AlexNet reduces the error rate to 16.4 %.
- **2015**—Computer vision sees breakthrough improvements. ResNet surpasses Human accuracy (5 % error rate) at 3.6 %, marking the start of an industry-wide AI boom.

AlexNet sparked a wave of progress in computer vision. In the years that followed, as seen in Figure 5.3, error rates kept falling. By 2015, models were achieving error rates below 5 %, outperforming humans on some image recognition tasks. Today, top systems routinely surpass human accuracy, identifying images with extraordinary precision.

The ImageNet breakthrough revealed several key lessons:
- **Data is essential:** Large, well-labeled datasets like ImageNet are the foundation of machine learning.
- **Computing power matters:** Advances in graphics processing units (GPUs) made it possible to train deep learning models efficiently.
- **Progress can be sudden:** After years of steady improvement, machine learning took a dramatic leap—showing how breakthroughs can reshape a field almost overnight.

This breakthrough helps explain why machine learning now powers tools and applications we once considered science fiction. It also sets the stage for understanding the main types of machine learning—and how they work.

To better understand the fundamental difference between traditional programming and machine learning, let's examine two simple yet illuminating examples.

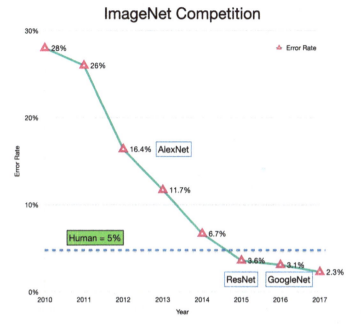

Figure 5.3: ImageNet Milestones. Timeline of the ImageNet Challenge highlighting major milestones that accelerated progress in artificial intelligence and computer vision, from its inception in 2006 to surpassing human-level accuracy in 2015.

Example 1: When Both Approaches Work

Consider a basic classification task: separating blue points from red points in a two-dimensional space, as shown in Figure 5.4. In this example, the points are arranged in a way that they can be separated by a straight line.

In this straightforward case, both traditional programming and machine learning can successfully classify the points. With the traditional programming approach, a developer would analyze the data, recognize the pattern, and then explicitly write an algorithm defining the boundary: "If a point falls above the line $y = 0.7x - 0.5$, classify it as red; otherwise, classify it as blue." This rule is hard-coded into the program, and the computer simply executes these instructions.

Similarly, with the machine learning approach, we provide the computer with the labeled data points (the "training data") and let it discover the pattern. The machine learning algorithm would automatically find the same linear boundary ($y = 0.7x - 0.5$) without being explicitly told what form the boundary should take. It learns this relationship directly from the examples.

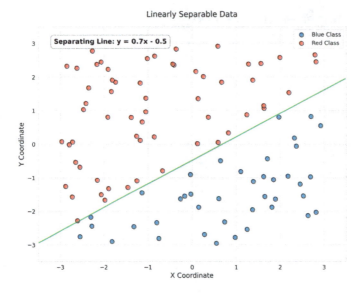

Figure 5.4: Linear Separability. Data points that can be separated by a linear boundary ($y = 0.7x - 0.5$). This two-dimensional example illustrates a case where both traditional programming and machine learning approaches work equally well. A programmer can identify and code the simple linear boundary explicitly, while a machine learning algorithm can discover the same boundary automatically from the training data. This linear separation represents the simplest case for classification problems, where the pattern is straightforward enough to be expressed as a simple mathematical formula.

While both approaches arrive at the same solution for this simple linear case, note the key difference: in traditional programming, the developer must identify and manually code the rule; in machine learning, the computer derives it automatically from the data. This distinction becomes crucial in our next example.

Example 2: When Traditional Programming Falls Short

Now, let's consider a more complex scenario where the blue and red points are arranged in a pattern that cannot be separated by a simple straight line, as shown in Figure 5.5.

With traditional programming (left panel), a developer would struggle to define a mathematical rule that accurately separates these points. They might try various approaches—perhaps a circular boundary or multiple linear boundaries—but the complexity quickly becomes unmanageable. Even if they eventually devise a rule (such as checking if a point's distance from the origin is less than some radius), it would likely be imperfect and fail to generalize well to new data points.

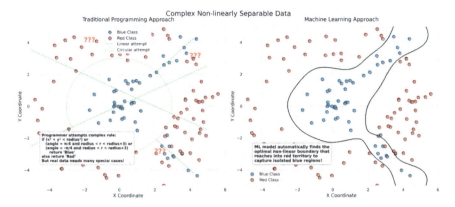

Figure 5.5: Beyond Linear Boundaries. Comparison of traditional programming versus machine learning approaches for non-linearly separable data with complex boundary shapes. Machine learning automatically discovers and models the tentacle-like extensions in the decision boundary without requiring explicit programming.

With machine learning (right panel), we simply provide the same labeled examples, and the algorithm automatically discovers a complex, non-linear boundary that effectively separates the classes. The computer doesn't need to be told what mathematical form the boundary should take—it learns this directly from the data.

This example highlights a crucial advantage of machine learning: it can uncover complex patterns that would be difficult or impossible to express through explicit programming rules. While this two-dimensional example is still comprehensible to human observers, real-world machine learning problems typically involve hundreds or thousands of dimensions where it becomes impossible for humans to visualize or manually program the boundaries separating multiple categories. As data complexity and dimensionality increase, traditional programming approaches become increasingly impractical, while machine learning continues to excel by automatically discovering the appropriate decision boundaries regardless of the dimensionality.

The Key Insight

These examples highlight the fundamental shift in how problems are solved with machine learning:

- **Traditional programming** relies on developers understanding the problem and coding rules by hand. It works well when the rules are clear and can be precisely defined.

- **Machine learning** enables computers to learn patterns from data, without requiring humans to specify the rules. It's especially useful for complex, dynamic problems where the patterns are too subtle or intricate to define explicitly.

As problems grow more complex—whether it's recognizing objects in images, interpreting language, or detecting user behavior—machine learning becomes more powerful. Instead of coding every possibility, we provide examples and let the system learn the underlying structure.

From Simple Examples to Tacit Knowledge

While our examples use visual patterns that are relatively easy to describe, machine learning truly shines when dealing with patterns that humans recognize intuitively but struggle to articulate explicitly. This is the realm of *tacit knowledge*—knowledge we possess but can't easily put into words or formal rules.

Consider how effortlessly we recognize a friend's face in a crowd, detect sarcasm in someone's tone of voice, or sense when a piece of music feels "right." We perform these complex pattern recognitions instantly, drawing on intuitive understanding that defies simple algorithmic description. A traditional programmer attempting to codify these intuitions would face an impossible task—not because of mathematical complexity alone, but because the knowledge itself resists formal expression.

Machine learning offers a powerful alternative approach. Rather than requiring humans to translate their tacit knowledge into explicit rules, it allows computers to learn directly from examples, much as humans do. By observing thousands of instances, the algorithm can discover subtle patterns and relationships that we ourselves might use unconsciously but cannot articulate precisely.

This ability to capture tacit knowledge makes machine learning particularly valuable in domains like natural language understanding, artistic style recognition, or medical diagnosis, where expert practitioners often rely on years of experience and intuition that goes beyond what can be expressed in a rulebook. The machine doesn't need to be told "why" a particular pattern exists—it simply learns to recognize the pattern itself from the examples it has seen.

5.3 Types of Machine Learning

Machine learning is often grouped into three main types: **supervised learning**, **unsupervised learning**, and **reinforcement learning**. Each one learns in a different way, depending on how the data is structured and what kind of feedback the system receives.

In this book, we'll focus mainly on **supervised learning**, as it forms the foundation for many real-world applications.

Supervised Learning: Learning from Labeled Examples

In supervised learning, a system learns from examples where the correct answer is already known. It's like using flashcards labeled "cat" or "dog" to teach a child. Over time, the system learns to map inputs (like images or text) to the right outputs.

Consider how we might teach someone to identify various fruits. We could show them multiple examples of apples, oranges, and bananas, each clearly labeled. After seeing enough examples, they learn to recognize the distinctive characteristics of each fruit: apples are typically round and red or green, oranges are round and orange with a textured skin, and bananas are elongated and yellow with a curved shape. Supervised learning works similarly—the machine examines thousands of labeled examples until it can reliably identify patterns that distinguish one category from another.

This method works well when we have historical data with clear outcomes—such as past loan approvals, labeled emails ("spam" or "not spam"), or medical test results. It's widely used in credit scoring, fraud detection, and disease diagnosis. The key advantage is that the system can learn to make predictions that mimic expert human judgment, often scaling to volumes of data no human could process.

Unsupervised Learning: Finding Hidden Patterns

Unsupervised learning works without labeled examples. The system is simply given raw data and asked to make sense of it. It looks for structure—groupings, patterns, or relationships—without being told what to look for.

Imagine arriving in New York City for the first time, without a map or guidebook. As you explore, you start to notice distinct neighborhoods forming naturally: Greenwich Village with its artistic atmosphere, narrow streets, and jazz clubs; the Financial District with towering skyscrapers and suited professionals; Chinatown with its vibrant markets and authentic restaurants; and the Upper East Side with its museums and upscale boutiques. Without anyone labeling these areas for you, you'd naturally begin to group streets and blocks based on their common characteristics—architecture styles, types of businesses, the pace of life, even the way people dress. That's unsupervised learning—figuring out the structure of data by noticing patterns, without any predefined labels. The city becomes organized in your mind into these natural clusters.

Another everyday example is how we might organize our wardrobe. Without anyone telling us which clothes go together, we naturally group items by type (shirts, pants, dresses), by color, by season, or by occasion (casual, formal, athletic). The groupings emerge naturally from the characteristics of the items themselves. Similarly, unsupervised learning algorithms can examine customer purchase data and identify natural groupings of shoppers based on their buying habits, even without being told what these groups should be.

This kind of learning is often used to explore data, segment customers into groups, detect unusual behavior, or uncover hidden trends in markets. It's about discovery rather than prediction. Businesses use it to understand their customer base better, identify market segments they hadn't explicitly defined, or spot anomalies that might indicate fraud or equipment failures.

Reinforcement Learning: Learning by Trial and Error

Reinforcement learning is about learning by doing. An "agent" interacts with its environment, makes decisions, and receives feedback in the form of rewards or penalties. Over time, it learns which actions lead to better outcomes.

Picture a robot in a maze. It tries different paths. When it hits a wall, that's a penalty. When it finds the exit, that's a reward. The robot keeps adjusting until it learns the best route. Reinforcement learning works the same way—learning by exploring and adjusting based on results.

This approach is similar to how we might learn a new skill like cooking. Initially, we might make mistakes—adding too much salt or overcooking pasta. But with each attempt, we gauge the results (how the dish tastes) and adjust our approach. Gradually, through this feedback loop of trying, evaluating, and adjusting, we improve our cooking skills. We don't need someone to give us the perfect recipe upfront; we discover what works through experience.

Reinforcement learning is useful when decisions build on each other, like driving a car, managing inventory, or playing a game. It's also key in fine-tuning large AI models. For example, reinforcement learning with human feedback helps align model responses with what users prefer. It can also be used in *distillation*, where a smaller model learns to act like a larger one by being rewarded for producing useful or similar responses.

Unlike supervised learning, which needs many examples with correct answers, reinforcement learning can work in situations where we know what a good outcome looks like overall (winning a game, safely reaching a destination) but don't necessarily know the best action at each step along the way. This makes it particularly valuable for complex sequential decision-making problems.

Conclusion

Machine learning changes how we think about solving problems. Instead of programming every rule, we train systems to learn from data. Traditional programming is powerful when the rules are clear. But many real-world problems—like recognizing speech, spotting fraud, or personalizing recommendations—are too complex to hard-code. That's where machine learning excels.

The ImageNet breakthrough showed what's possible when we combine large datasets, powerful algorithms, and modern computing. It marked the start of a new era—one where machines don't just follow instructions, they learn from experience.

In the next two chapters, we'll focus on supervised learning through two case studies: one on regression, the other on classification.

6 Classification: Predicting Categories (Case Study)

No man is equipped for modern thinking until he has understood the anecdote of Agassiz and the sunfish.

—Ezra Pound

Classification is one of the most widely used techniques in machine learning. It involves predicting a category or class label for each new input based on patterns learned from past data. Some problems involve multiple categories—such as identifying objects in images (cat, dog, airplane, etc.), as in the ImageNet competition discussed in the previous chapter. Others are binary, such as predicting whether a customer will default on a loan.

In this chapter, we focus on binary classification: problems with two possible outcomes. For example: Is this email spam? Will this customer buy our product? Should we approve this loan?

We'll explore this topic through a case study: how a regional bank might use machine learning to support loan decisions. The goal is to understand how a model can learn from past approvals and denials and apply that knowledge to new applicants.

6.1 Problem Statement

Verona Savings and Loan (VSL) is a fictitious regional bank used for this case study. For years, VSL has relied on experienced loan officers to review applications, assess applicants' finances, and make loan decisions.

As the bank expands into new cities, the volume of applications is rising quickly. With limited staff and a commitment to high-quality service, VSL faces a clear challenge: how to handle growing demand without compromising decision quality.

This is where machine learning enters the picture. VSL's Board has asked the CEO to develop a predictive model to streamline loan processing. Can a model trained on past decisions help predict outcomes for new applicants? Could it support loan officers—or even automate part of the process?

Fortunately, the bank has detailed records of past applications, including applicant data and final decisions. These records provide a foundation for training a model that reflects the judgment of experienced professionals.

https://doi.org/10.1515/9783111583549-009

Case Study Summary

Problem: Loan application volume is rising faster than VSL's capacity to review them manually.
Solution: Build a machine learning model trained on historical loan decisions to optimize the review process.

In the sections that follow, we walk through VSL's journey step by step—demonstrating how classification models work and how they can be applied to real-world decision-making.

6.2 Supervised Machine Learning Model Development Workflow

Before we build VSL's loan decision model, let's review how supervised machine learning works. In this approach, we train a model using labeled examples—data where the correct answer is already known. The model learns from these examples and applies what it learns to make predictions on new, unseen cases.

Think of it like learning from a teacher: you're shown problems with solutions, then tested on similar problems later.

Throughout this book, we use a simple five-step process for explaining how to build supervised learning models (Figure 6.1):

1. **Define and prepare the data.** Identify the outcome to predict (the *target variable*) and the input information used to make that prediction (the *feature variables*). Data must often be cleaned—fixing errors, handling missing values, or reshaping it into usable form.

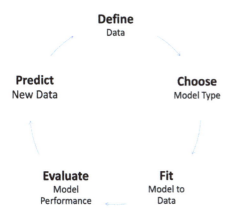

Figure 6.1: Supervised Learning Workflow. An iterative process moving through data definition, model selection, fitting, evaluation, and prediction. The cycle is often iterative, with later insights informing earlier steps.

2. **Choose a model type.** Some models are simple (like linear regression); others are more complex (like deep learning). Each has trade-offs. In this chapter, we use K-Nearest Neighbors—a model that's easy to understand and visualize.
3. **Fit the model to the data.** Fitting adjusts the model to reflect patterns in the data. This is where learning happens—when the model identifies relationships it can use to make future predictions.
4. **Evaluate the model.** We test how well the model performs by comparing its predictions to known outcomes. The evaluation metrics depend on the task—classification uses different measures than regression.
5. **Use the model to make predictions.** Once trained and tested, the model is ready to help us make informed decisions on new data.

These steps form a cycle. As we gather insights, we often revisit earlier decisions—adjusting the data, trying a different model, or refining how we measure success. The process is iterative, not linear.

For VSL, we'll follow this five-step path—starting with how the team prepared their data.

6.3 Step 1: Prepare the Data

Like most machine learning projects, VSL's effort begins with data—not with a model. Over the years, the bank has kept detailed records of past loan applications, including financial information about each applicant and whether the loan was approved or denied. This historical data forms the foundation for training a model that can generalize from past decisions to new ones.

Each application is represented as a row in a table, and each column captures a specific piece of information. These columns fall into two types. The target variable is what the model is trying to predict—in this case, whether the loan was approved or denied. The feature variables are the inputs used to make that prediction, such as the applicant's income or credit score.

Preparing the data means more than assembling a table. It requires cleaning errors, filling in missing values, and understanding which variables matter. At VSL, data scientists worked with experienced loan officers to decide which features best captured meaningful patterns. For this case study, they settled on three: income, measured as annual earnings; credit score, ranging from 0 to 800; and loan status, a binary outcome—1 for approved, 0 for denied (Table 6.1).

An astute reader might wonder why only two features are being used when loan decisions often involve many factors. The answer lies in a key principle of machine learning: simpler models are usually better—at least to start. Fewer inputs make the model easier to explain, which matters in regulated industries like banking. Simpler

Table 6.1: Sample of the training data. The model uses income and credit score to predict loan status (1 = approved, 0 = denied).

Income	Credit Score	Status
74,637	511	0
132,564	610	1
106,113	588	1
85,149	556	0
100,279	575	1

models also train and deploy more quickly, and they're less likely to overfit—that is, to memorize training data instead of learning general patterns. And of course, collecting fewer variables reduces costs and maintenance overhead.

As shown in Figure 6.2, plotting the data reveals patterns that a table alone can't show. Applications with higher income and credit score tend to be approved; those with lower values tend to be denied. But there's no crisp boundary—just trends. This kind of subtlety is where machine learning excels.

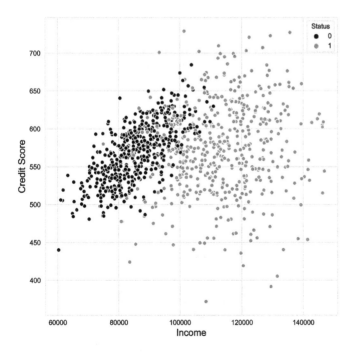

Figure 6.2: Loan Decisions by Income and Credit Score. Scatterplot showing loan applications by income and credit score. Approved loans appear in grey, denied loans in black.

With the data now cleaned, selected, and visualized, VSL is ready to move on to choosing a model.

6.4 Step 2: Choose the Model

With the data now prepared and visualized, VSL moves to the next step in the supervised learning workflow: choosing a model.

There are many models to choose from. Some rely on advanced mathematics; others are easier to interpret. Since our goal is understanding, VSL selects a method that's simple, visual, and intuitive—K-Nearest Neighbors (KNN).

Why KNN?

KNN works by example. It doesn't build abstract rules or optimize complex equations. Instead, it predicts outcomes by looking at similar cases from the past. This approach mirrors how people often reason—using memory and similarity.

To illustrate, imagine trying to predict how a new resident of a neighborhood will vote. We don't know their views, but we know how their neighbors voted in the last election. If most nearby voters chose one party, we might guess the new person will do the same. KNN uses a similar principle. If three out of five "nearby" applicants were approved for loans, the model will likely predict approval for a similar new applicant.

Common Classification Models

Many machine learning tasks can be framed as classification problems. Below is a summary of widely used classification models—each with its own strengths, assumptions, and ideal use cases.

Logistic Regression Estimates the probability of a binary outcome using a weighted combination of inputs. Simple, interpretable, and often a strong baseline.

Decision Trees Creates a flowchart-like structure of decisions based on input values. Easy to interpret but can overfit without pruning.

Random Forest An ensemble of decision trees that improves accuracy by averaging predictions. Reduces overfitting and handles a variety of data types.

Support Vector Machine (SVM) Finds the boundary that best separates classes in high-dimensional space. Effective for structured data where clear margins exist.

K-Nearest Neighbors (KNN) Predicts outcomes based on the majority class among the most similar past examples. Simple and intuitive; ideal for teaching and exploration.

Naive Bayes A fast probabilistic model based on Bayes' theorem. Assumes feature independence and works well for text classification and spam detection.

Neural Networks Models that learn complex relationships through layers of interconnected nodes. They form the foundation of deep learning—a topic we'll explore later in the book.

How KNN Works

Each loan application in VSL's dataset becomes a point on a two-dimensional map, defined by income and credit score. When a new application arrives, the model locates the most similar past applications—its "nearest neighbors"—and uses their outcomes to make a prediction.

The number of neighbors considered by the model is called K. If $K = 3$, the model looks at the three closest points. If two were approved and one denied, it predicts approval. If $K = 5$, it takes a broader sample.

This approach is both flexible and easy to understand. It handles ambiguity naturally: if a new application falls in a dense cluster of approvals, the prediction is clear. If it lands in a mixed or "border" zone, the prediction may shift depending on the value of K.

For this case study, VSL sets $K = 3$—a small number that keeps the model responsive while avoiding overfitting to any one example.

With the model type selected and K defined, the team is ready for the next step: fitting the model to the data.

Step 3: Fit the Model to the Data

With the model selected, it's time for VSL to teach it how to make predictions. This step is called fitting the model—and it's where machine learning gets its name. The model "learns" by studying past data and identifying patterns it can use to make future predictions.

For KNN, this step is unusually simple. Unlike many models that adjust weights or optimize equations, KNN does not build an internal formula. Instead, it stores the training data—past loan applications—so it can refer back to them when making predictions.

You can think of KNN as a memory-based system. When a new application comes in, the model compares it to past cases and asks: "Which of these are most similar? And what were their outcomes?" This is why KNN is sometimes called lazy learning—it doesn't generalize upfront. It waits until a prediction is needed before doing the work of comparison.

Despite its simplicity, KNN can be surprisingly effective. In VSL's case, each application is described by two features: *income* and *credit score*. To compare applications, the model calculates the distance between them. Applicants with similar values will be closer together; those with very different values will be farther apart.

The most common measure of this distance is Euclidean distance—the straight-line distance between two points.

How KNN Measures Similarity: Euclidean Distance

To compute the distance between two points A and B:

With two features (e. g., income and credit score):

$$d(A, B) = \sqrt{(x_1 - x_2)^2 + (y_1 - y_2)^2}$$

With n features:

$$d(A, B) = \sqrt{(a_1 - b_1)^2 + (a_2 - b_2)^2 + \cdots + (a_n - b_n)^2}$$

or more compactly:

$$d(A, B) = \sqrt{\sum_{i=1}^{n}(a_i - b_i)^2}$$

The smaller the distance, the more similar the two applicants.

Once the data is stored and the distance formula defined, the model is ready to make predictions. No further training is required. That's one of the advantages of KNN: it's simple to set up and quick to apply—especially with smaller datasets like VSL's.

With the model fitted, the next step is to test how well it performs.

Step 4: Evaluate the Model

Once the model is fitted, the next question is: How well does it perform?

To answer this, VSL uses a *test set*—data the model hasn't seen before. The model makes predictions on these cases, and the results are compared to actual outcomes.

These results are summarized in a tool called a **confusion matrix** (Figure 6.3), which classifies predictions into four outcomes:

- **True Positives (TP):** The model predicted approval, and the loan was approved.
- **True Negatives (TN):** The model predicted denial, and the loan was denied.
- **False Positives (FP):** The model predicted approval, but the loan was denied.
- **False Negatives (FN):** The model predicted denial, but the loan was approved.

This structure is widely used—not only in finance but also in medicine, public health, and security systems.

For $K = 3$, VSL's KNN model achieves an accuracy of 0.93.

The team also generates a **classification report** (Figure 6.4) to analyze further: The report includes two key metrics:

- **Precision:** When the model predicts approval or denial, how often is it correct?
- **Recall:** Of all the actual approvals or denials, how many did the model catch?

The **F1-score** combines both into one number. In VSL's case, the model performs well across both outcomes.

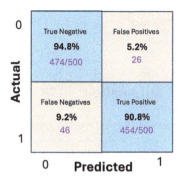

Figure 6.3: Confusion Matrix for $k = 3$. The model correctly classifies most applications, with slightly more false negatives (9.2 %) than false positives (5.2 %).

```
                 precision    recall  f1-score   support

             0       0.91      0.95      0.93       500
             1       0.95      0.91      0.93       500

      accuracy                           0.93      1000
     macro avg       0.93      0.93      0.93      1000
  weighted avg       0.93      0.93      0.93      1000
```

Figure 6.4: Classification report for $k = 3$. The F1-score is 0.93 for both approval and denial categories, indicating balanced performance.

Step 5: Predict New Data

Once trained and evaluated, the model is ready for real-world use.

At VSL, this means using the model to assess incoming loan applications. When a new applicant submits their income and credit score, the model compares this data to past applications and predicts whether the loan should be approved or denied.

During the pilot, the bank takes a cautious approach. Every prediction is reviewed by a loan officer before a final decision is made.

The workflow is as follows:

1. Applicant information is entered.
2. The model finds the distance to prior cases.
3. It identifies the $K = 3$ nearest neighbors.
4. It checks the majority outcome.
5. It makes a prediction.
6. A loan officer reviews the result.
7. The prediction and final decision are recorded.

This setup allows VSL to monitor real-world performance and build trust in the system.

Human-in-the-Loop: Scaling with Smart Automation

As confidence in the model grows, VSL begins to scale. They introduce a system that separates *solid predictions*—high-confidence results—from *edge cases* that still require human review.

To support this, VSL begins using models that return *probability scores*, such as logistic regression.

– Predictions with probability 80 % or greater are approved automatically.
– Predictions with probability 30 % or lower are rejected automatically.
– Predictions in the intermediate zone are flagged for human review.

During the pilot, 100 % of applications required human review. Now, only 50 % require human review. Loan officers can focus on complex decisions, while routine ones are handled automatically (Figure 6.5).

With time, VSL can adjust the thresholds and retrain the model to improve further. But human oversight remains—especially for high-stakes or ambiguous decisions.

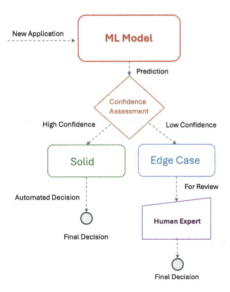

Figure 6.5: Human-in-the-loop Workflow. The model predicts outcomes, but only uncertain cases are reviewed by experts.

Conclusion

In this chapter, we explored how machine learning can support decision-making through a case study at Verona Savings and Loan. Using KNN, we followed the supervised learning process: preparing data, choosing a model, fitting it, evaluating its performance, and making predictions. We saw how KNN works by comparing new cases to past examples. We evaluated model performance with confusion matrices and F1-scores. And we showed how automation can be combined with human judgment to create reliable, scalable systems.

Good data is the foundation. Simpler models can be powerful. And machine learning works best when it complements rather than replaces human decision-making.

Next, we turn to regression, where the goal is to predict numeric values. Our next case study asks: Does sleep improve academic performance?

7 Regression: Predicting Continuous Values (Case Study)

The best thing about being a statistician is that you get to play in everyone's backyard.

—John Tukey

In the previous chapter, we explored classification— where the goal is to predict categories. Our focus was on binary classification, such as predicting whether a loan should be approved or denied. But classification also applies to multi-class settings, where the model predicts which of several possible categories applies—for example, the likely reason a customer might cancel a subscription or which department should handle a support request.

This chapter turns to a different kind of prediction: estimating a quantity. Instead of choosing between categories, we want to predict a number—how much, how many, how high. How much will sales increase? How many units will sell? What score will a student receive on an exam? These kinds of problems require regression.

Where classification predicts type, regression predicts magnitude. It models relationships between variables to estimate how one changes in response to another. To explore how this works, we'll use a practical example: Does getting more sleep the night before improve a student's performance on their final exam? If so, by how much?

To answer this question, we'll use Multiple Linear Regression (MLR). Like K-Nearest Neighbors, MLR builds on an intuitive idea: outcomes often result from several factors, each making its own contribution. MLR helps quantify those contributions to make an overall prediction.

We'll follow the same supervised learning process introduced earlier—preparing data, selecting a model, fitting it, evaluating performance, and making predictions—but now we'll apply it to a continuous outcome rather than a categorical one.

7.1 Problem Statement

A team of faculty and university researchers wants to understand what factors influence students' performance on final exams. They're especially interested in a common piece of advice: getting more sleep the night before an exam improves performance. To test this idea, they design a research study and collect data on a large group of students.

https://doi.org/10.1515/9783111583549-010

> **Case Study Summary**
>
> **Problem:** A research team wants to know whether getting more sleep the night before an exam improves performance on the final exam.
> **Solution:** Use multiple linear regression model trained on real student data to predict final exam performance based on a number of variables, including sleep.

In the sections that follow, we'll walk through the team's process step by step—showing how regression models can help quantify relationships, predict outcomes, and offer practical insights for students and educators alike.

7.2 Step 1: Prepare the Data

As with most machine learning projects, the work begins with data—not with a model. The research team collects information from more than two thousand students. For each student, they record several pieces of information that might affect exam performance: the student's GPA entering the course, the number of hours spent studying for the final exam, the number of hours of sleep the night before, and parental income. The outcome they want to predict—the *target variable*—is the final exam score, measured on a 0 to 100 scale.

Table 7.1: Sample of student performance data. The goal is to predict the final exam grade based on the other variables.

GPA	Income	Sleep	Time	Grade
2.9	82,461	6.5	47	77
3.7	61,113	6.2	47	94
2.8	63,632	6.2	39	69
2.0	66,854	7.2	49	81
2.8	82,721	5.5	49	78

Each row in Table 7.1 represents one student. The other pieces of information are called features: they are the input variables used to make predictions. For example, GPA may reflect how well a student has done in previous courses. Study time tells us how much effort the student put in for this exam. Sleep captures short-term rest and recovery. Parental income may relate to the broader context of a student's educational experience.

Exploratory Data Analysis

Before training any model, the team takes time to explore the data in detail. This step is called *exploratory data analysis*, or EDA. It's an essential part of any machine learning project. The goal is to understand what the data looks like, how the variables behave, and whether there are any surprises, errors, or patterns worth noticing.

The team begins by asking simple but important questions: Are there missing values? Are all the numbers within expected ranges? Do the distributions of variables—like sleep or study time—seem reasonable? Are there students who studied 100 hours or slept only one hour? These checks help flag possible errors or outliers.

They also create visualizations, like histograms and scatterplots, to see how variables are spread out and how they might relate to one another. The goal of EDA is to help the team build intuition about the relationships in the data.

Another goal of EDA is to make sure that each feature is contributing something unique. If two features are highly correlated—for example, if students who sleep more consistently study more (or less) in a predictable pattern—then including both might introduce redundancy and could potentially harm model performance due to multicollinearity. But in this case, the team finds that GPA, sleep, and study time each offer different information about performance, which is a good sign for building a useful model.

With the data reviewed, visualized, and better understood, the team is ready to move on to the next step: choosing a model.

7.3 Step 2: Choose the Model

With the data prepared and understood, the next step is to choose a model. Since the goal is to predict a number—a student's final exam score—the team selects a method called *Multiple Linear Regression*.

This type of model is commonly used when several factors might influence an outcome. It takes a set of input variables—called **feature variables**—and estimates how each one contributes to a numerical result, known as the **target variable**.

7.4 A Theoretical Interlude

To motivate the selection of MLR as the model type, let's embark on a theoretical interlude and consider the distinction between *correlations* and *causes*.

The real world is a world of causation. A virus causes disease. Capital investment causes company growth. Force causes acceleration. Meanwhile, artificial intelligence, including machine learning models, inhabit the shadowy and inferior world of correlations. At first glance, this appears to be a major drawback. Science, after all, not only describes *how* things are, but explains *why* things are the way they are. A chasm separates artificial intelligence as correlation from science as causation.

Here MLR comes to the rescue by giving us a partial reprieve. In this chapter, we will call upon MLR to do double duty. Our primary goal is still prediction: we can *predict y*, without knowing what *causes y*. But our secondary goal is to anticipate causal analysis. We will see that MLR is a powerful tool for making predictions, but it also provides an initial glimpse into the structure of causality. Although causal analysis is outside the scope of this book, since it is not yet a strict part of artificial intelligence, a solid understanding of multiple regression provides an essential background for later study of causality. Multiple regression also provides a foundation for understanding the structure of deep learning models.

Accordingly, we begin our study of MLR by assuming a highly *simplified causal picture* of the world. We wish to understand how some effect *e* arises. Our simplified causal picture makes four basic assumptions. Our first assumption states that for any effect *e*, there are multiple *possible* causes: $c_1, c_2, \ldots, c_n$. This first assumption, as illustrated in Figure 7.1, conforms to our ordinary notion of causality. A one-to-one cause-effect relationship is rare. A many-to-one cause-effect relationship is more common. In statistics, a possible cause is also referred to as a *covariate*.

Our second assumption states that each cause acts *independently* of the others. In the real world, this assumption is frequently violated. Causes quite often conspire together to bring about an effect. Two criminals work together to rob a bank. Several musicians, along with a conductor, perform a symphony. Genes and environment work in tandem to produce traits or phenotypes. Models that take into

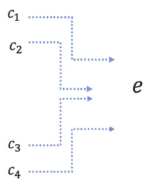

Figure 7.1: Multiple Causes, One Effect. Illustration of a simplified causal picture in which an effect *e* arises from multiple possible causes (c_1, c_2, c_3, c_4). This reflects the common many-to-one structure of real-world causal relationships.

account interactions between causes are called *additive* or *interactive models*. But in our simplified world, we will assume that causes are entirely solitary creatures, acting upon the effect wholly independently of other causes.

Our third assumption states that causes *vary* in their contribution to the effect. Some causes play a stronger role while others play a weaker role in bringing about an effect. I am sad today because it is raining *and* I lost my favorite book. What is the greater cause of sadness? Is it the fact that it is raining, my having lost a prized book, or some combination of both?

We can capture the strength of the cause by associating a multiplicative weight (w). The causes that contribute more to bringing about the effect have higher weights, and those which contribute less have lower weights. The multiplicative weight of each cause is illustrated in Figure 7.2.

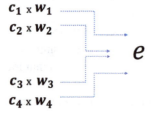

Figure 7.2: Weighted Contributions of Causes. Causes vary in the strength of their influence on an effect. In linear models, this variation is captured by assigning each cause a multiplicative weight, with higher weights indicating stronger contributions.

Our final assumption states the *overall* effect is simply the weighted sum or *linear combination* of the causes. A linear combination is a type of aggregation. Instead of taking a simple sum, we calculate a weighted sum. In mathematics, a linear combination is constructed from a set of terms by multiplying each term by a constant and adding the results. In our case, the terms are the variables representing the causes and the constants are the corresponding weights.

$$\textbf{effect} = w_1 c_1 + w_2 c_2 + \cdots w_n c_n$$

To complete the picture, we also add a bias term b to the weighted sum. This is for technical reasons that need not concern us here.

$$\textbf{effect} = w_1 c_1 + w_2 c_2 + \cdots w_n c_n + b$$

If we rewrite the equation using standard variables x and y, where x stands for cause and y stands for effect, and weights are expressed with β, then we arrive at the fundamental equation for multiple regression:

$$\text{MLR Equation: } y = \beta_0 + \beta_1 x_1 + \beta_2 x_2 + \cdots \beta_n x_n \tag{7.1}$$

The MLR equation elegantly summarizes the four assumptions. Conceptually, we think of the effect simply as the weighted sum of the contributions of the causes. This approach to modeling has several advantages. First, we are able to *separate* out each cause and examine its specific contribution to the effect. As a practical matter, we want to understand *that* a cause influences some effect. But we also want to understand *how much* that cause influences the effect. This is achieved with the weight or coefficient in the MLR equation.

Second, multiple regression models are interpretable. In AI, for most models we can't peer inside the "black box" to examine how the prediction is generated. But with MLR models, we have the advantage of transparency when it comes time to interpret and explain our models. Transparency is a critical aim of model development, especially when our models have to be explained to stakeholders.

Third, multiple regression belongs to the family of *linear models*. Why is this important? Linear models have well-understood mathematical properties that make them ideal for a variety of use cases.

In summary, we have explicated multiple regression in two ways. From the standpoint of prediction, the target variable y is a linear combination of the feature variables $x_1, x_2, \ldots, x_n$. From the standpoint of causality, the effect is a linear combination of the causes.

Identify Predictor and Target Variables

As part of the research design, the researchers hypothesize that a number of variables, along with sleep, are likely to affect exam performance. Which additional variables? Certainly, *student ability* is likely to play a role. Better students perform better than poorer students. The quality of the *instructional environment* is also likely to matter. A student is more likely to learn in a supportive environment. Also, the *amount of time* a student studies or practices for the exam is also likely to play a role in improving the final exam grade.

The researchers have developed a preliminary list of possible causes, covariates, or "suspects" of academic performance. We now come across our first hurdle. Each of our variables has to be measurable. Measuring the quality of the instructional environment, for example, is complex. It's not easily measurable, since it is a function of teacher quality, curriculum quality, the time allocated for instruction, and so on. In such complex cases, we can sometimes resort to a useful stratagem: we introduce a *proxy variable*. A proxy is something that stands in for something else. Since instructional quality is difficult to measure, we can try employing *parental income* as a proxy. In our study, we will use parental income as a *proxy* for the quality of instructional environment. Our supposition is that wealthier students will have access to more instructional resources and opportunities than poorer students. Proxy variables can be handy but they should always be used guardedly, since we might be smuggling in unknown assumptions.

Along with sleep and parental income, we will include two other variables in our study. The first is study time: the number of hours a student spent studying for the exam. Second, we include each student's incoming grade point average (GPA). Here again, we are resorting to a proxy variable. Student ability, which should influence academic performance, is once again complex and difficult to measure. We hypothesize that GPA can serve as a proxy for student ability. Figure 7.3 summarizes the prediction structure for the MLR case study.

Figure 7.3: Predictors of Exam Performance. Sleep, study time, GPA, and parental income are treated as possible causes—or covariates—of a student's final exam grade. The figure also illustrates the use of proxy variables, such as parental income for instructional quality and GPA for student ability, in cases where direct measurement is difficult.

We have settled, therefore, on four independent variables or features for our multiple regression model: *Sleep, Time, GPA*, and *Income*. Through multiple regression, we aim to predict final exam grade based on these four feature variables.

7.5 Step 3: Fit the Model to the Data

Now that the model has been chosen and the structure defined, the next step is to fit the model to the data. This is the point where learning happens—where the model examines real examples and figures out the best values for the coefficients.

In MLR, fitting the model means finding the set of weights (β values) that make the predicted exam scores as close as possible to the actual scores in the dataset. The model looks at each student's inputs—GPA, sleep, study time, and income—and adjusts the weights so that the resulting predictions match the real grades as closely as possible.

This process uses a well-established method called *least squares*. The idea is simple: the model calculates how far off each prediction is from the true grade, squares that difference (so that large errors count more), and adds up all the squared errors. It then adjusts the coefficients to minimize this total. In other words, the model searches for the line (or surface, in higher dimensions) that best fits the data.

The math behind this process is handled automatically by statistical or machine learning software. What's important to understand is the goal: to learn a relationship between inputs and outcomes that is both accurate and interpretable.

Initial Results

Once trained on the data, the model produces a specific equation:

Learned Model After Fitting

$$\text{Grade} = -39.7 + 9.10 \times \text{GPA} + 0.000006 \times \text{Income} + 7.21 \times \text{Sleep} + 1.06 \times \text{Time}$$

Each coefficient now has a concrete value that tells us how much that feature contributes to the predicted grade:
- A one-point increase in GPA adds about 9 points to the predicted exam score.
- Each additional hour of sleep is worth about 7.2 points.
- An extra hour of study time adds about 1 point.
- Income has a very small effect: even large increases in income change the prediction by only a fraction of a point.

These results suggest that GPA, sleep, and study time are the main drivers of exam performance in this dataset. Income appears to contribute very little.

Refining the Model

After reviewing the results, the team checks whether each feature passes a statistical test. This test helps answer the question: *Is the relationship we see real, or could it have happened by random chance?*

Parental income fails this test—it does not show a statistically reliable relationship with exam grades. In other words, the model cannot say with confidence that income has any real impact on the outcome. In this context, we think of the statistical test as an alibi for a suspect. Parental income has an "alibi" and is not implicated as a possible cause of performance in the final income.

Accordingly, the team decides to remove income from the model for two reasons. The first reason is that it didn't pass the test for statistical significance. Secondly, even if it had, its contribution to the final grade is negligible. They retrain the model using only GPA, sleep, and study time.

Refined Model Without Income

Grade = −39.7 + 9.10 × GPA + 7.21 × Sleep + 1.06 × Time

With the model now trained and refined, the next step is to evaluate its performance on new, unseen data.

7.6 Step 4: Evaluate the Model

Once the model is trained, the team needs to assess how well it performs. The goal is to answer a basic but important question: *How accurate are the predictions?*

To evaluate the model, the team tests it on new data that wasn't used during training. These are real students whose outcomes are known, but hidden from the model. The model makes predictions for these students, and the team compares those predictions to the actual exam scores.

Performance Metrics

Two key metrics help summarize how well the model performs:
- **Root Mean Squared Error (RMSE):** This tells us, on average, how far off the predictions are from the actual grades. In this case, the RMSE is about 4.8 points—meaning that the model's predictions are typically within about 5 points of the real score.
- **R-squared (R^2):** This measures how much of the variation in student grades the model is able to explain. An R^2 value of 0.89 means that 89 % of the differences in exam scores can be accounted for using GPA, sleep, and study time.

In a social science context, where many factors influence outcomes, an R^2 of 0.89 is unusually high. It suggests the model captures a substantial portion of what drives exam performance.

Correlation, Causation, and Standards of Evidence

When interpreting regression models, it's critical to remember that R^2 and other metrics measure correlation strength, not causal relationships. This distinction parallels different standards of evidence in legal systems:

Multiple Linear Regression (R^2) is like the standard in *civil cases*: "preponderance of evidence" (more likely than not). When variables show strong correlation, we have suggestive evidence of a relationship, but not definitive proof of causation.

Causal inference, on the other hand, requires a standard closer to *criminal cases*: "beyond reasonable doubt." This demands controlled experiments, addressing confounding variables, and often specialized techniques like instrumental variables or natural experiments.

Multiple linear regression can be valuable as a stepping stone toward causal understanding, but moving from correlation to causation requires additional evidence and methodological rigor. When a business leader asks, "What happens if we increase X?" they're asking a causal question—one that regression alone cannot definitively answer without additional causal inference techniques.

For leaders making decisions, understanding this distinction is crucial. Regression analysis can identify patterns and suggest hypotheses, but causal claims require stronger evidence and more sophisticated analytical approaches.

Interpreting the Regression Equation

The model produces numbers—called **coefficients**—that describe how much each feature contributes to the prediction. These coefficients are based on the original units of measurement (GPA points, hours of sleep, etc.) and are called *non-standardized coefficients*.

We can interpret the regression coefficients as follows: For each unit of increase in GPA, final exam score increases on average by 9.10 points; each additional hour of sleep increases final exam score by 7.21 points; and one hour of additional study time leads to a 1.06 point gain on the final exam.

It appears that *GPA* leads to the biggest gains. However, we have to be careful because our variables have different units. As is, the coefficients are not comparable in terms of their influence on the outcome variable. However, there is a way to make the coefficients comparable. The topic of standardizing coefficients in regression is beyond the scope of this book. For those who are interested, we examine the topic on the book's website.

We make another observation of practical significance. Some independent variables can't be changed. *GPA* is the incoming grade for the student. It can't be changed by the student during the course. By contrast, both *Sleep* and study *Time* are *actionable*. This means that an instructor can provide feedback to students *during the course*. What the study shows is that there are clear benefits to sleeping more the night before and studying consistently during the duration of the semester. Not only are there benefits, but we have precisely quantified the gains through multiple regression.

7.7 Step 5: Predict New Data

With the model trained and evaluated, the team is now ready to use it. The goal is to apply what the model has learned to make predictions for new students—students whose final exam scores are not yet known.

Making Specific Predictions

Suppose a new student has the following profile:
– GPA: 3.0
– Sleep: 7 hours the night before the exam
– Study time: 50 hours

Using the refined model, the predicted grade is:

Example Prediction

$$\text{Grade} = -39.7 + 9.10 \times (3.0) + 7.21 \times (7) + 1.06 \times (50) = 91$$

This student is predicted to score a 91 on the final exam—well above average. The model combines the effects of GPA, sleep, and study time to generate this result.

Understanding Trade-offs

Beyond predicting a single number, the model can also help students and educators think about trade-offs. For example, if a student is deciding between studying an extra hour or going to bed an hour earlier, the model suggests that sleep might have the larger benefit: one additional hour of sleep is associated with about a 7-point increase in predicted score, compared to about 1 point for an extra hour of study.

But these numbers should be interpreted within the constraints of the model. Our linear regression represents an approximation of the relationship within the observed range of our data. The model can help identify relative importance (sleep appears more impactful than study time in this dataset), but may not capture the full complexity of extreme scenarios or values outside our observed data range.

The real power of the model lies in helping students make informed choices—especially when time and energy are limited. It doesn't give hard rules, but it does offer evidence-based guidance.

With the ability to make predictions and explore trade-offs, the model can now serve as a tool not just for understanding, but for decision-making.

7.8 Step 6: Human-in-the-Loop—Applications in Education

The insights from the regression model can be valuable for both students and educators—but only when used thoughtfully. Like any tool, the model works best when paired with human judgment.

For Students

Students can use the model to make more informed decisions about how to prepare for exams. The model suggests that consistent study time is strongly associated with better performance, while getting enough sleep the night before the exam appears to provide a significant benefit. The data also shows that entering the course with strong preparation (as captured by GPA) matters, but students can still improve outcomes through focused effort and rest. This kind of feedback may help students better allocate their time—especially in the final days before a test—by showing where their efforts are likely to have the greatest impact.

For Educators

Educators can also use the model to inform instructional design and student support. The findings suggest educators might benefit from emphasizing the importance of rest and recovery alongside preparation, and designing course schedules that allow students time for review rather than compressing deadlines. The model highlights that student success is shaped by multiple, interacting factors—some of which may fall outside the classroom. Recognizing these diverse influences can help educators develop more holistic approaches to supporting student achievement.

7.9 Conclusion

In this chapter, we explored how regression models can be used to predict continuous outcomes—in this case, students' final exam grades. Unlike the classification model in the previous chapter, which produced yes-or-no decisions, our regression model generated specific numerical predictions.

We began by framing the problem: can more sleep before an exam improve performance? To answer this, we used real student data and built a regression model that included GPA, study time, and sleep as feature variables. Parental income was also included at first, but later removed when it showed no meaningful contribution.

We saw how Multiple Linear Regression works: it fits a simple equation that combines weighted contributions from each feature. The model learned those weights by minimizing prediction error across thousands of examples. Once trained, it offered not just predictions, but insight—showing which variables matter most, and how much they matter.

We also discussed how students and educators can use the model to support decision-making, while recognizing its limits. Models simplify reality. They highlight patterns, but they don't capture everything.

Part IV: **Deep Learning**

8 Deep Learning: The Big Picture

The perceptron is designed to illustrate some of the fundamental properties of intelligent systems in general, without becoming too deeply enmeshed in the special, and frequently unknown, conditions which hold for particular biological organisms.

—Frank Rosenblatt

It's no coincidence that today's most advanced AI systems are inspired by the human brain. After all, the brain is nature's most powerful learning machine. This chapter introduces **artificial neural networks**, often referred to as **deep learning**—the technology behind many of the AI tools that we now use every day. From voice assistants that understand our questions to apps that recognize faces or generate lifelike images and text, deep learning is the engine driving it all.

We begin by exploring the biological inspiration for these systems and trace how early computer scientists looked to the brain for clues about building machines that could learn. From there, we shift our focus to how neural networks work in practice as **prediction machines**. To make this idea more tangible, we will use a mechanical analogy to explain a neural network's inner workings. Finally, we will break down the five key principles that underlie most deep learning models, laying a clear foundation for everything that follows.

8.1 Neural Networks in Biology and Early AI

The human brain forms an intricate network of about 86 billion specialized cells called neurons. (See Figure 8.1.) Biological neurons communicate through junctions known as *synapses*, sending electrical and chemical signals to one another. When a neuron receives enough input from its neighbors, it fires an electrical impulse down its *axon*, passing the message along to other neurons. This core process—receiving signals, processing them, and sending responses—drives everything the brain does, from basic reflexes to our most complex thoughts, emotions, and behaviors.

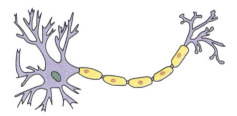

Figure 8.1: Biological Neuron. Wikicommons. License under Creative Commons CC0.

https://doi.org/10.1515/9783111583549-012

This biological architecture inspired the first formal model of artificial neural networks in 1943, when neuroscientist Warren McCulloch and logician Walter Pitts published a groundbreaking paper proposing that the brain could be understood as a computational system (McCulloch and Pitts, 1943). They argued that brain activity could be described using the tools of mathematical logic. Their model featured artificial neurons that received binary ("all or none") inputs, applied simple logical rules, and produced binary outputs. Their key insight was that, when linked together in networks, these simple units could perform any computation that could be described using formal logic. Although their model couldn't capture the full complexity of the brain, it introduced the powerful idea that thought, memory, and behavior might emerge from networks of simple computational elements.

The next major step came in 1958, when psychologist Frank Rosenblatt introduced the **perceptron**, a type of neural network that could learn from data (Rosenblatt, 1958). Unlike McCulloch and Pitts' fixed design, Rosenblatt's model could adjust the strength of the connections—what we now call *weights*—between artificial neurons. This ability to adapt made it possible to recognize simple patterns like letters or shapes. Although the perceptron had clear limits (it could only solve problems that were linearly separable, as Marvin Minsky and Seymour Papert later showed), it was an important advance (Minsky and Papert, 1969). It introduced the idea of *learning from experience*—a core principle in today's deep learning systems.

Prediction Machines

Now that we've looked at the biological roots of neural networks, let's shift perspectives to better understand how these systems work in practice. Instead of neurons and synapses, imagine a machine composed of interlocking gears, as depicted in Figure 8.2. This serves as our prediction machine. Data goes in, the gears turn, and out comes a prediction.

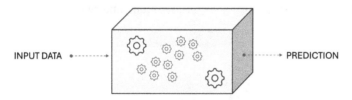

Figure 8.2: The Deep Learning Prediction Machine. A conceptual illustration of a neural network as a system of interlocking gears. Each gear represents a component that helps transform input data into an output prediction.

This metaphor isn't as far-fetched as it might seem. The earliest "thinking machines" were mechanical, built by pioneers like Gottfried Wilhelm Leibniz and Charles Babbage using gears, levers, and cogs. Today's neural networks run on silicon chips, not brass, but the gear-based analogy still gives us a useful way to picture how they process information.

Traditional machine learning models can also be viewed as prediction machines, albeit simpler ones. They typically consist of a few gears—parameters—that have been carefully designed and tuned by human experts. These models are effective for tasks where the relationships in the data are relatively straightforward and well-understood.

In contrast, deep learning models are "mega prediction machines," comprising millions or even billions of gears. These vast networks can automatically learn complex patterns from large amounts of data, making them well-suited for tasks like image recognition, natural language processing, and other applications involving unstructured data. The sheer scale and complexity of these models enable them to capture intricate relationships that simpler models might miss.

Neurons

At the core of the prediction machine are neurons—the basic processing units, inspired by brain cells. An artificial neuron works like a tiny machine with its own set of gears. (See Figure 8.3.) It receives several inputs, processes them, and produces a single output. When millions—or even billions—of these atomic computing units are connected in a network, they can solve surprisingly complex problems.

Figure 8.3: An Artificial Neuron as a Machine. Illustrated as a gear-based unit, the artificial neuron receives multiple inputs, processes them through a weighted mechanism, and produces a single output. It serves as the basic building block of deep learning systems.

Artificial neurons are highly simplified versions of real neurons in the brain. A biological neuron either fires or stays inactive depending on the combined strength of its inputs. In much the same way, an artificial neuron takes in inputs and applies a set of simple rules to produce an output. Its internal setup—the way its "gears" are arranged—determines how it transforms inputs into outputs. During the training phase, the configuration of gears is adjusted step by step, allowing the network to improve over time.

Layers

In a deep learning network, neurons are organized into layers. The process begins with the input layer, which holds the raw data—such as an image or a set of numbers. This layer doesn't contain any neurons; it simply serves as the starting point for the network. Next come one or more hidden layers, which contain neurons that process the data step by step. Finally, the output layer produces the network's prediction. (See Figure 8.4.)

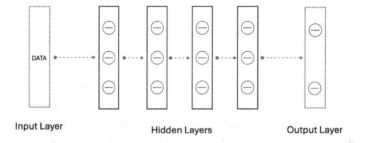

| Input Layer | Hidden Layers | Output Layer |

Figure 8.4: Layers of a Neural Network. A simplified neural network architecture showing the flow of data from the input layer, through several hidden layers containing neurons, to the output layer where the prediction is made. Most of the computation happens in the hidden layers.

We can think of the layers like runners in a relay race. Each layer takes the data, transforms it, and passes it to the next. The final runner—the output layer—crosses the finish line with the prediction.

Forward Propagation

Forward propagation is the process by which a neural network turns raw input into a final prediction. Data flows from the input layer through the hidden layers and ends at the output layer. At each stage, the network identifies more complex patterns in the data.

In an image recognition task, as shown in Figure 8.5, the input might be a grid of raw pixel values. The first layer might detect simple features like edges or corners. The next layer combines those features into shapes—curves, rectangles, or outlines.

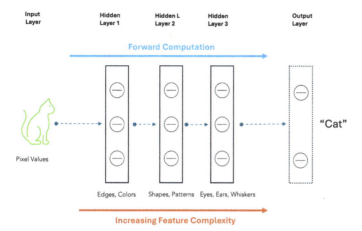

Figure 8.5: Forward Propagation in a Neural Network. An illustration of how data flows through a deep learning model from left to right, transforming raw input (e. g., an image of a cat) into increasingly abstract and complex features at each layer, ultimately producing a prediction.

As the data moves deeper into the network, these shapes become parts of objects: eyes, ears, whiskers. By the time the signal reaches the final layer, the network has enough information to say, "this is a cat."

Each neuron contributes to this step-by-step transformation. Like gears in a machine, the neurons process what they receive and pass a refined version of the data forward. Layer by layer, the network builds a deeper understanding of what it sees.

Loss Function

Once the machine makes a prediction, we need a way to measure how far off it is from the correct answer. That's the role of the loss function—a kind of metaphorical error meter that shows how close or far the prediction is from the truth.

The loss function compares the network's prediction to the correct result and calculates an error score. For example, if the network predicts a house is worth $400,000 but the actual value is $450,000, the error is $50,000. In a classification task, if the network gives only a 55 % chance that an image is a cat when "cat" is the correct label, the loss function penalizes it for being unsure. (See Figure 8.6.)

Smaller errors mean better predictions. The loss becomes a key signal that tells the machine how well it's doing—and how it needs to improve. This feedback is what drives learning.

Figure 8.6: Learning from Error: The Loss Function. In a house price prediction task, the neural network processes property features to produce a predicted price of $400,000. The true price is $450,000, resulting in a prediction error—or loss—of $50,000. This loss guides the network during training, helping it adjust its internal parameters to improve future predictions.

Back Propagation

So far, we've seen how a neural network takes in data, processes it through layers of neurons, and produces a prediction. We've also introduced the loss function, which measures how far that prediction is from the correct answer. But knowing the error isn't enough—the real question is: *How does the machine get better?*

That's where **backpropagation** comes in. This is the key step that allows a neural network to learn. Backpropagation is a feedback loop that fine-tunes the machine's internal gears based on the error from the last prediction.

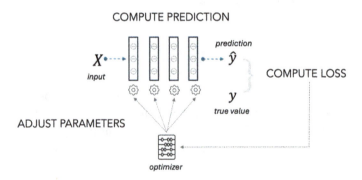

Figure 8.7: The Learning Cycle in a Neural Network. Input data (X) passes through the network during forward propagation to produce a prediction ($\hat{y}$). This prediction is compared to the true value (y) to compute the loss. The optimizer then adjusts the network's parameters—weights and biases—using backpropagation to reduce the error. This feedback loop is repeated millions or even billions of times during training, gradually improving the model's accuracy.

Imagine a skilled mechanic reaching into the machine after each run, making tiny adjustments based on how it performed. Backpropagation works like that. It traces the error backward through the network, nudging each gear—each weight—in just the right direction. If the prediction was too low, it makes small tweaks to push the next prediction a little higher. (See Figure 8.7.)

Historical Note: The Rise of Backpropagation

Backpropagation—the algorithm that allows neural networks to learn from their mistakes—was first introduced by Paul Werbos in his 1974 doctoral thesis (Werbos, 1974). But it wasn't until the 1980s that it gained widespread attention, thanks to the work of Geoffrey Hinton, David Rumelhart, and Ronald J. Williams (Rumelhart et al., 1986). Their 1986 paper showed how backpropagation could effectively train multi-layer neural networks, reigniting interest in neural computation and laying the groundwork for today's deep learning revolution.

Geoffrey Hinton

These adjustments are tiny—just a fraction of a turn on each gear—but they're precisely calculated to reduce the error. That's why the machine needs to see many examples, over and over. With each cycle—forward propagation, error calculation, and backpropagation—the network learns a little more.

Over time, the gears settle into configurations that consistently produce accurate results. Like a muscle strengthened through repetition, the network becomes more skilled with each run, eventually performing with impressive accuracy.

8.2 The Five Pillars of Deep Learning

Now that we've explored the prediction machine through a mechanical lens, let's step back and identify the core principles that make it work. While gears and levers help us visualize deep learning in action, five foundational ideas apply to all neural networks—regardless of their architecture or purpose.

The diagram below highlights these five essential elements: neurons, layers, forward propagation, the loss function, and back propagation. These are the five pillars of deep learning. Whether you're building a basic image classifier or a cutting-edge language model, these principles remain central to how learning happens.

In the next chapter, we'll examine the technical details behind each component. For now, a clear understanding of these high-level ideas provides a strong foundation for everything to come.

Principle 1: *A neuron is the atomic computational unit of a deep learning network.*

Just as atoms form the building blocks of matter, neurons form the basic units of a neural network. Each neuron performs a simple operation: it receives multiple inputs, computes a weighted sum (plus a bias), and applies a nonlinear transformation to produce an output. The weights and biases act like adjustable gears—when tuned correctly, they allow the neuron to respond to meaningful patterns in the data.

Principle 2: *Neurons are organized in a set of connected layers.*

Neurons don't work in isolation. They're arranged into layers, each passing information to the next. The input layer receives raw data. Hidden layers transform that data step by step, and the output layer produces the final prediction. While the input layer simply passes information along, the hidden and output layers contain the learnable parameters that make learning possible.

Principle 3: *Forward propagation through the layers is the computational process for generating predictions.*

To make a prediction, the network pushes data forward through its layers in a process called forward propagation. Each neuron applies its weights and biases to the incoming signals, producing outputs that become inputs for the next layer. This chain of transformations—from raw data to meaningful predictions—is what gives deep learning its power. The "depth" of the network refers to how many layers participate in this process, allowing the system to learn increasingly abstract and complex features.

Principle 4: *A loss function measures the error by comparing the prediction against the true value.*

Once the network makes a prediction, it needs to know how far off it was. That's the role of the loss function. It compares the prediction to the correct answer and returns an error score. This score becomes essential feedback. Different tasks use different loss functions—for example, predicting house prices requires a different measure than classifying photos—but in every case, the loss guides the learning process.

Principle 5: *Backward propagation is the learning process by which the network adjusts its parameters.*

After calculating the loss, the network needs to learn from its mistakes. Backward propagation—often shortened to backprop—does exactly that. It moves the error signal backward through the network, calculating how much each weight and bias contributed to the final error. Then it updates these parameters in small, precise steps. Over time, this feedback loop allows the network to refine its predictions. While the basic idea is simple, implementing it at scale is what makes deep learning both powerful and challenging.

8.3 Conclusion

Deep learning may rely on massive data and computation, but at its core, it runs on a few simple, elegant ideas. By thinking of neural networks as prediction machines—with neurons as gears, layers as assembly lines, and learning as iterative refinement—we've built an intuitive understanding of how these systems function.

The five principles introduced in this chapter form the conceptual backbone of deep learning. They apply across tasks, models, and domains—from recognizing cats in photos to generating paragraphs of human-like text. As we move forward, we'll explore how these pillars work in practice and why they've proven so effective.

You don't need to memorize the math or master every detail just yet. What matters is the big picture: deep learning systems are designed to make predictions, and everything they do—from adjusting weights to refining outputs—serves that single goal.

In the next chapter, we'll zoom in on the neuron: how it performs its computation, and how networks of neurons learn to model patterns far more complex than any one neuron could handle on its own.

9 Deep Learning: Under the Hood

We describe a new learning procedure, back-propagation, for networks of neurone-like units.

—David E. Rumelhart, Geoffrey E. Hinton & Ronald J. Williams

In the previous chapter, we introduced five foundational ideas that make deep learning possible: neurons, layers, forward propagation, the loss function, and backpropagation. In this chapter, we take a closer look at each one—examining how they work individually and how they fit together.

The Neuron

To understand neural networks, we start with their smallest unit: the neuron. Let's develop a precise intuition about how a neuron works. As we move forward with our intuition, we will sprinkle in some formalism. The mathematics is remarkably simple, mostly addition, multiplication, and division. To make this abstract concept more concrete, let's use an analogy.

Imagine a junior analyst named Max. He will be our stand-in for the work done by a neuron. Max works at an organization that recommends which car brands and models to buy. His job is to analyze specific cars and reach a judgment. He's not the final decision maker, but his opinion will be passed along to someone higher up.

Max forms his recommendation in three steps. First, he weighs the advice he receives, giving different importance to each source. Next, he forms an overall judgment, adjusting for any biases he detects in the group's opinions. Finally, he calibrates how strongly to express his recommendation, deciding whether to speak cautiously or with full confidence based on the clarity of the evidence (Figure 9.1).

Figure 9.1: A Neuron at Work: Max the Analyst. Max consults a team of advisors, weighs their input, adjusts for bias, and calibrates the strength of his recommendation. This mirrors how an artificial neuron processes inputs, applies weights and a bias, and passes the result through an activation function to produce an output.

https://doi.org/10.1515/9783111583549-013

Step 1: Weigh Advice

To begin, Max consults a group of advisors: a mechanic who evaluates reliability, a safety expert who reviews crash ratings, a financial advisor who considers cost and value, an efficiency specialist who analyzes fuel economy, and a family friend who is a car hobbyist.

Max doesn't treat all opinions equally. He weighs each advisor's input differently, depending on the car under consideration. Sometimes, the mechanic's view might carry more weight; at other times, cost might be the deciding factor, so the financial advisor's opinion matters more. The family friend's anecdotal advice might count for less, though not always.

Max combines the inputs, giving more weight to some and less to others. That's exactly how an artificial neuron works—it adjusts each input by weighing its importance. After weighing the inputs, Max adds them up.

Step 1: Weigh Advice

Suppose Max receives five inputs about a car from his advisors (x_i) and attaches corresponding weights (w_i). See Figure 9.2. Max computes the weighted sum by multiplying each input by its corresponding weight:

$$z = w_1 x_1 + w_2 x_2 + w_3 x_3 + w_4 x_4 + w_5 x_5$$

Substituting values for the example:

$$z = (0.4)(8) + (0.3)(9) + (0.1)(6) + (0.15)(7) + (0.05)(5) = 7.8$$

In general, if there are n inputs, the weighted sum is written as:

$$z = \sum_{i=1}^{n} w_i x_i$$

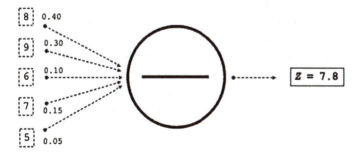

Figure 9.2: Computing the Weighted Sum. A visual representation of a neuron receiving five inputs $(x_1$ to $x_5)$ along with their respective values and weights. The neuron multiplies each input by its corresponding weight, adds the results, and produces the weighted sum $z = 7.8$. This step models how a neuron integrates multiple sources of information to produce an intermediate output.

Or more compactly, using vector notation and the dot product:
$$z = \mathbf{w} \cdot \mathbf{x}$$
This step is just multiplication and addition.

Step 2: Form Judgment

Having calculated the weighted sum, Max now forms an overall judgment about the advisors' collective input. Maybe this particular team tends to be overly cautious, or maybe they tend to underrate certain kinds of cars. To account for this tendency, Max applies a final adjustment—a small nudge up or down to correct for any systematic bias in the group's advice.

In a neural network, this adjustment is called the **bias**.

Step 2: Form Judgment

After calculating the weighted sum z, Max adds a bias term b to adjust the result:
$$z = \sum_{i=1}^{n} w_i x_i + b$$
Using our earlier example:
$$z = 7.8 + b$$
If $b = 0.5$, then:
$$z = 8.3$$
The bias allows the neuron to shift its decision boundary—just like Max adjusting the team's recommendation based on experience or context.

Step 3: Calibrate Recommendation

Max doesn't simply pass along his adjusted judgment as-is. He calibrates how strongly to make his recommendation. If the advisors' inputs are uncertain or conflicting, he might hold back. If the evidence is clear and consistent, he might express his recommendation with greater confidence. This final calibration shapes not just whether he recommends the car, but how forcefully he does so.

In a neural network, this final shaping rule is called the **activation function**. It determines how the neuron responds to different levels of input—whether by suppressing weak signals, amplifying strong ones, or filtering the output into a specific range.

We can think of the activation function like a *filter* or *volume knob*. It controls the strength of the neuron's output. Sometimes it mutes weak signals; sometimes it lets strong signals pass through unchanged. It's this final shaping that gives the network its flexibility and expressive power.

And crucially, activation functions introduce **non-linearity** into the system. Without them, even deep networks would collapse into a single linear equation. The activation function is what enables neural networks to learn complex, curved, and layered patterns in data.

Step 3: Calibrate Recommendation

After computing the adjusted score z, the neuron applies an activation function $\phi(z)$ to produce the final output:

$$a = \phi(z)$$

A commonly used activation function is ReLU (Rectified Linear Unit)), defined as:

$$\phi(z) = \begin{cases} z & \text{if } z > 0 \\ 0 & \text{if } z \leq 0 \end{cases}$$

In plain terms: ReLU passes through positive values unchanged, and blocks negative values by outputting zero. It acts like a gate—letting strong signals through, silencing the rest.

For example:
- If the adjusted score is $z = 8.3$, then: $a = \phi(8.3) = 8.3$
- If $z = -2$, then: $a = \phi(-2) = 0$

ReLU is widely used because it is simple, fast to compute, and introduces the non-linearity essential for deep learning.

Max's process—consulting advisors, weighing their input, forming an overall judgment, and calibrating his recommendation—captures exactly how an artificial neuron works. Of course, in real deep learning systems, a neuron isn't weighing five opinions—it may receive input from tens of thousands, even millions, of other neurons. That's where the simplicity of the neuron's rule becomes powerful: even though each one performs a simple calculation, when you connect many of them together, they can handle astonishingly complex patterns.

But Max is not alone. In a deep learning system, there are millions of Maxs—each one a junior advisor, quietly processing signals and passing recommendations forward. They are the workhorses of deep learning networks. And when we connect them together—layer upon layer—they become more than the sum of their parts. That's where the real power begins.

9.1 Layers

Neural networks are organized in layers, stacked one after another. Each layer contains multiple neurons and plays a specific role in processing information (Figure 9.3).

- The first layer is the **input layer**, where raw data enters the network. This layer doesn't perform any computation—it simply passes the input features forward.

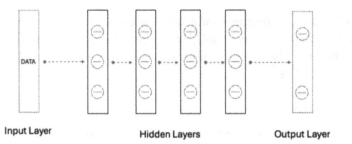

Input Layer   Hidden Layers   Output Layer

Figure 9.3: Layered Structure of a Neural Network. A simplified architecture showing an input layer that receives raw data, multiple hidden layers where the data is transformed, and an output layer that produces the final prediction. Each layer plays a specific role in the flow of information through the network.

For example, in an image, each pixel value might be assigned to a different node in the input layer.

- The real work begins in the **hidden layers**. These layers transform the data step by step. A network is considered "deep" when it includes several hidden layers stacked together. They're called "hidden" because they sit between input and output—we don't see their workings directly, but they're responsible for most of the learning.
- Finally, the **output layer** delivers the result—whether it's a prediction, classification, or recommendation. For a classification task, the output might be a category like "cat" or "dog." For a regression task, it might be a number like a predicted price.

Connections Between Layers
Neurons in one layer typically connect to every neuron in the next. These links carry outputs from one layer to serve as inputs for the next—forming the communication lines of the network. When each neuron in a layer is connected to all neurons in the next, we call it a **dense** or **fully connected** layer.

A Simple Network Example
Let's make this concrete. Imagine a toy network (Figure 9.4) with three layers:
- An input layer with 3 values.
- A hidden layer with 4 neurons.
- An output layer with 2 neurons.

Each neuron in the hidden layer receives all 3 inputs, requiring $3 \times 4 = 12$ weights. Each also has a bias term, adding 4 more parameters. That's 16 parameters for the hidden layer.

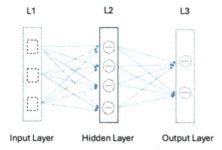

Figure 9.4: A Fully Connected "Dense" Neural Network. A toy example with 3 input nodes, 4 neurons in a single hidden layer, and 2 neurons in the output layer. Each neuron is fully connected to all nodes in the previous layer. The network contains a total of 26 parameters: 20 weights and 6 biases.

Each neuron in the output layer receives inputs from all 4 hidden units, for $4 \times 2 = 8$ weights, plus 2 biases. That gives 10 parameters.

In total, this small network has $16 + 10 = 26$ parameters.

The Power of Depth

One of deep learning's greatest strengths is its ability to build layered representations. Early layers detect simple features—edges in images or individual tones in sound. As data flows forward, each layer builds on the last. Mid-level layers might recognize shapes, textures, or object parts. Deeper layers identify full concepts—like faces, trees, or sentiment in text.

By stacking many simple processing steps, deep networks can solve complex problems with surprising accuracy. This layered structure is what allows neural networks to learn patterns in images, text, speech, and more.

Hyperparameters

The weights and biases of a neural network are called **parameters**. These are learned automatically during training.

Other values—such as the number of layers, number of neurons per layer, activation function, or choice of loss function—are not learned. These are called **hyperparameters**. They define the architecture and behavior of the network and must be set manually. Choosing the right hyperparameters is a crucial part of building effective models.

How Many Parameters for a Layer?

Suppose we have two layers in a dense neural network:
- Layer L_1: n neurons
- Layer L_2: m neurons

Each neuron in L_2 receives one input from every neuron in L_1, requiring $n \times m$ weights. Each neuron in L_2 also has its own bias term. That adds m more parameters.

Thus, the total number of parameters needed to define Layer L_2 is:

$$\text{Parameters} = (n \times m) + m$$

To compute the total number of parameters in the full network, apply this formula to every pair of connected layers and sum the results.

Note: As networks grow deeper and wider, the number of parameters can grow quickly. (Table 9.1) This gives neural networks their expressive power—but also increases the data and computation needed to train them effectively.

Table 9.1: Comparison of Large Language Models.

Model	Type	Estimated Layers	Parameters	Release Date
GPT-3	Proprietary	96	175 billion	June 2020
GPT-4	Proprietary	Est. 120	Est. 220B-1T+	March 2023
DeepSeek LLM	Open Source	70	67 billion	January 2024
Gemini Ultra	Proprietary	Not disclosed	Est. 500B-1T+	December 2023
Claude 3 Opus	Proprietary	Not disclosed	Est. 175B-500B	March 2024

9.2 Forward Propagation

Once a neural network is structured with layers of connected neurons, it needs a way to turn input into output. This step-by-step transformation process is called **forward propagation**.

Forward propagation describes how information flows through the network—from the input layer, through each hidden layer, to the output layer. It's a one-way journey with no loops or backward steps. In standard feedforward networks, each layer passes its result to the next, refining the data at every stage.

We can think of forward propagation like an assembly line. Raw materials, the input data enters at one end. Each layer acts as a station that performs a specific transformation. By the time the data reaches the end of the line, it has been reshaped into a prediction.

In an image recognition system, for example, the input might be raw pixel values. The first layer may detect basic features like edges. The next layer might recognize shapes or patterns. Later layers begin to assemble these parts into whole objects—a paw, a face, a cat. The deeper the network, the more abstract the representation becomes. This gradual transformation—from low-level detail to high-level concept—is what gives deep learning its power (Figure 9.6).

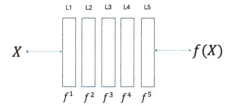

Figure 9.5: Forward Propagation as Nested Functions. The diagram shows how a neural network applies a series of functions (f^1 through f^5) in sequence. Each function represents a layer that transforms its input and passes the result forward, creating a nested computation where each output becomes the input to the next layer.

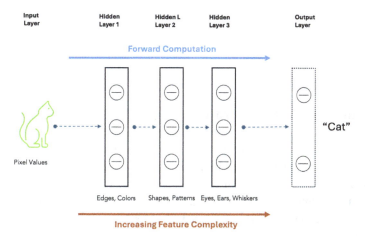

Figure 9.6: Forward Propagation in a Neural Network. Information flows from input layer (left) through hidden layers to output layer (right). As data progresses (blue arrow), the network detects increasingly complex features (orange arrow)—from pixels to edges, shapes, recognizable features, and finally classifications like "cat".

Each layer does something simple, but when we stack enough of them, the network can uncover patterns too complex to define manually. That's why forward propagation is at the heart of what makes deep learning effective.

Forward Propagation as Function Composition

Note: Don't worry if the math looks complex—the key idea is that information flows through the network one layer at a time.

Each layer in a neural network can be thought of as a function. Forward propagation is the process of applying these functions one after another—passing the result of one layer as input to the next. This process is called **function composition** (Figure 9.5).

If we have five layers represented by functions f^1, f^2, f^3, f^4, f^5, and an input X, the network's output is:

$$f(X) = f^5\left(f^4\left(f^3\left(f^2\left(f^1(x)\right)\right)\right)\right)$$

Each function f^i represents one layer: apply weights and biases, then pass the result through an activation function.

A Simple Example:
- $f(x) = x + 1$
- $g(x) = 2x$
- $h(x) = x^2$

Apply to $x = 3$:

$$h\left(g\left(f(3)\right)\right) = h\left(g(4)\right) = h(8) = 64$$

Each layer performs a small transformation. When stacked, these simple operations produce rich and complex results. This is the essence of forward propagation.

9.3 The Loss Function

Once a neural network produces an output, it faces a key question: *How good was that prediction?* The answer comes from the **loss function**.

The loss function acts like a scorekeeper. It compares the network's prediction to the correct answer and returns a single number: the **loss**. The loss is the same as **error**. The loss function measures how far off the prediction was from the intended target. A perfect prediction earns a small loss; a bad prediction earns a large one. This number tells the network during training how well it's doing and how much it needs to improve.

Imagine a network in training to predict house prices. If it estimates a house at $300,000 but the actual sale price is $350,000, it's made a mistake. We can measure that mistake in a few different ways—just taking the difference ($50,000), or the absolute value (ignoring whether the guess was too high or too low). Another option is to square the difference, which makes larger mistakes count even more. For tasks like predicting prices, it's common to use this squared approach, since it makes the math work out nicely and puts more weight on big errors. This is called the **mean squared error**, and it's one of the most popular ways to help the network learn from its mistakes.

The Loss Function: Measuring Error

The loss function compares the network's prediction to the correct value and returns a single number that represents the error.

Example: House Price Prediction

$$\text{Actual price} = 350{,}000$$
$$\text{Predicted price} = 300{,}000$$
$$\text{Error} = 350{,}000 - 300{,}000 = 50{,}000$$

A common loss function for regression is the **Mean Squared Error (MSE)**. For one prediction:
$$\text{Loss} = (50{,}000)^2 = 2.5 \times 10^9$$

In practice, the network predicts many examples at once. The loss function computes the average error across all of them:

$$\text{MSE} = \frac{1}{n} \sum_{i=1}^{n} (y_i - \hat{y}_i)^2$$

Where:
- y_i is the true value
- $\hat{y}_i$ is the predicted value
- n is the number of examples

Different tasks use different loss functions, but all serve the same purpose: to quantify how far off the network is—and guide it to do better.

Loss functions matter for three reasons. First, they guide learning. Without a way to measure error, the network has no direction. Second, they help track progress. During training, we expect the loss to decrease if the model is improving. And third, they're task-specific. Whether we're predicting numbers, classifying images, or generating text, the loss function defines what "better" means.

Most importantly, the loss function forms the bridge between prediction and learning. Once the network sees how wrong it was, it can start adjusting its internal parameters to reduce that error. This kicks off the feedback loop that drives training: *predict → evaluate → adjust*. Without a loss function, the network would be flying blind.

Loss functions matter for three reasons. First, they guide learning. Without a way to measure error, the network has no direction. Second, they help track progress. During training, we expect the loss to decrease if the model is improving. And third, they're task-specific. Whether we're predicting numbers, classifying images, or generating text, the loss function defines what "better" means.

Most importantly, the loss function forms the bridge between prediction and learning. Once the network sees how wrong it was, it can begin adjusting its internal parameters to reduce that error. This kicks off the feedback loop that drives training: **predict → evaluate → adjust.** Without a loss function, the network would be flying blind.

9.4 Backpropagation

So far, we've seen how a neural network makes a prediction and how the loss function measures its error. But how does the network actually learn? How does it use that error to improve?

The answer is **backpropagation**. This is the feedback mechanism that allows the network to adjust itself based on how well—or how poorly—it performed.

We can think of a neural network like a complex machine made of gears. Forward propagation runs the machine: inputs go in, layers turn their gears, and out comes a prediction. Afterward, we check how far off that prediction was using the loss function. Then comes the key insight: we go back through the entire machine and ask, *How can we adjust each gear in the machine, in our case the set of weights and biases, to get a better prediction?*

Backpropagation is that backwards pass. It traces the error from the output layer all the way back to the earliest layers, adjusting each weight and bias slightly to improve performance the next time. In a real network, this can mean updating millions—or even billions—of parameters. Yet the basic idea remains the same: each one is nudged in the direction that would have reduced the error.

The changes are small. Each connection in the network is nudged—just a little— in the direction that would have reduced the error. Over many training examples, these tiny nudges add up. Like a musician practicing a difficult passage, the network gradually tunes itself toward better performance.

The important point is that learning happens through a systematic feedback loop. The network doesn't guess or explore randomly. Instead, a component called the **optimizer** uses the error signal from the loss function to compute precise adjustments to each weight and bias. These steps are small, but carefully calculated to reduce the error on the next prediction. Over time, these small changes accumulate— and the network gets smarter.

Backpropagation: How Learning Happens

Backpropagation updates each parameter in the network—like a weight or bias—based on how much it contributed to the prediction error.

This is done using the **gradient**, which tells us how sensitive the loss is to each parameter. Think of the gradient like a slope: it points in the direction we should move to reduce the loss most efficiently.

Each weight is updated using the following rule:

$$w \leftarrow w - \eta \cdot \frac{\partial L}{\partial w}$$

Where:
- w is a weight in the network,
- L is the loss (the error signal),

- $\frac{\partial L}{\partial w}$ is the gradient—the slope of the loss with respect to w,
- η (eta) is the **learning rate**, which controls how big the adjustment step is.

This update is applied to every weight and bias in the network. It's how the model learns from mistakes—by adjusting the connections that caused them.

You don't need to follow every symbol to understand the main idea: *backpropagation is the process of sending the error backward and using it to make small improvements, one step at a time.*

9.5 Conclusion

In this chapter, we've taken a deeper look inside the prediction machine. We've seen how deep learning systems turn raw input into intelligent output—not by following fixed rules, but by learning from data, one example at a time.

At the heart of it all are five core ideas that work together to make learning possible:

- **Neurons** are tiny decision-makers that weigh inputs, apply adjustments, and generate outputs.
- **Layers** organize neurons into a sequence—each one building on the last to detect increasingly abstract patterns.
- **Forward Propagation** pushes data through the network, producing a prediction based on what the system has learned so far.
- **The Loss Function** tells the system how far off its prediction was—a single number that measures the mistake.
- **Backpropagation** uses that mistake as feedback, guiding the network as it adjusts its internal settings to do better next time.

What makes deep learning powerful isn't just any one part, but the way these components work together in a feedback loop. The system predicts, evaluates, adjusts, and tries again. With each cycle, it learns a little more—and slowly, it builds up the ability to make smart, accurate decisions in complex environments.

Part V: **Generative AI**

10 Foundation Models: Large Language Model Basics

> Generative models are a key enabler of machine creativity, allowing machines to go beyond what they've seen before and create something new.
>
> —Ian Goodfellow

In this chapter, we will walk through the basics of building a Large Language Model (LLM) like ChatGPT. Understanding this process provides a practical lens for grasping how these models generate human-like text, where their strengths come from, and why they fail. By tracing the construction of an LLM from raw data to a functional system, we gain insight into its remarkable abilities, as well as its fundamental limitations. Our journey will unfold in five basic steps: assembling the **corpus**, defining the **vocabulary**, creating **embeddings**, **pre-training** with predictions, and refining behavior with **fine-tuning**. Each of these steps contributes to the model's ability to interpret and produce language, and together, they form the basis on which advanced capabilities are built.

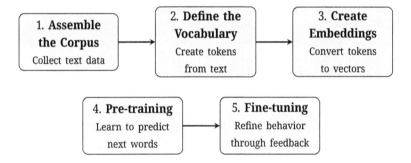

A Big Picture View

An LLM is among the most sophisticated systems in modern computing, built on cutting-edge advances in machine learning, algorithm design, and computer hardware. As we explore its inner workings, it is essential to keep in view the big picture: understanding the *fundamental principles behind its design* without getting lost in technical complexity.

With this framework in mind, let's consider a helpful analogy. To understand the basics of building an LLM, imagine the comparable process of running a world-class restaurant (Figure 10.1). Just as crafting an exceptional dish begins with sourcing high-quality ingredients, training an LLM starts with acquiring a *corpus*—the

https://doi.org/10.1515/9783111583549-015

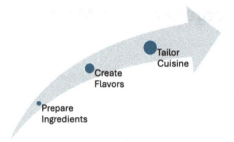

Figure 10.1: Restaurant-to-LLM Analogy. The basic steps in preparing cuisine at a world-class restaurant mirror the process of building a large language model, from sourcing ingredients to final refinement.

vast collection of text from which the model learns. But raw ingredients alone do not make a great meal; they must be carefully selected and prepared, much like defining the right *vocabulary* to ensure the model has the essential linguistic building blocks. Think of these first steps as prep work in the kitchen: assembling the ingredients and doing the basic work of cutting, chopping, and readying them for cooking.

Next comes the transformation process. Just as a chef skillfully blends ingredients to create rich flavors and textures, an LLM processes its raw text into *embeddings*—mathematical representations that capture the meanings and relationships between words. These embeddings function like a chef's deep understanding of how ingredients interact, allowing the model to interpret context, nuance, and subtle connections within language.

But having the finest ingredients and a deep understanding of flavors is not enough; overall execution is key. A master chef perfects their craft through practice, refining techniques with repeated trial and adjustment—just as an LLM undergoes *pretraining*, learning to predict and generate text by recognizing patterns in its vast dataset. This stage is comparable to a chef mastering fundamental cooking methods, ensuring consistency and refinement across various dishes.

Finally, just as a chef tailors a dish to suit the unique style of a restaurant and the preferences of its diners, an LLM undergoes *fine-tuning*. This process refines the model's responses based on specific tasks, user feedback, or ethical considerations, much like a chef making final adjustments to balance flavors to meet the expectations of a discerning clientele and the local community.

It's important to remember that these steps are not strictly linear. In both culinary artistry and model development, refinement is an iterative process—adjusting ingredients, tweaking techniques, and incorporating feedback to perfect the final product. By keeping this big picture in mind, we can better appreciate the complexity behind LLMs while maintaining a clear understanding of their fundamental design principles.

The Fundamental Mechanism: Prediction

At their core, Large Language Models (LLMs) operate on a deceptively simple principle: next-word prediction. Nothing more, nothing less. Every response, every para-
graph of fluid text, each response is the result of this single mechanism—repeated
over and over again.

We can think of this process as **"Next-Word Staircasing"**—each prompt and
prediction pair forms a step, and by iterating this process, a coherent passage of
text emerges (Figure 10.2).

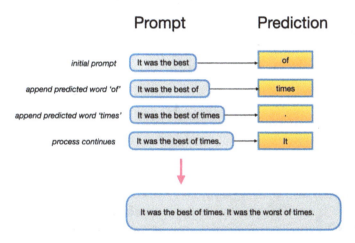

Figure 10.2: Next-Word Staircasing Process. Large Language Models generate text through sequential prediction, where each new word builds upon all previous words, creating coherent passages
step by step—illustrated here with the opening lines of Dickens' *A Tale of Two Cities*.

The process of generating text in an LLM follows a sequential approach. Starting with an initial prompt like 'It was the best', the model evaluates the context and
predicts the most probable next word—in this case, 'of'. This prediction is then appended to create a new extended prompt: 'It was the best of'. When fed back into
the model, this updated prompt generates another prediction—'times'—which is
again appended to form 'It was the best of times'. The process continues iteratively,
with each new word building upon all previous words, creating a step-by-step construction of text. Through this repetitive prediction mechanism, the model might
eventually produce the complete phrase 'It was the best of times. It was the worst
of times.', the famous opening line from Dickens' *A Tale of Two Cities*. Or, upon instruction from a user, the LLM might produce an entire chapter. At no point does the
model plan ahead to create this sentence; rather, each word emerges solely from

what came before it, demonstrating how coherent and contextually appropriate text can emerge from simple *next-word predictions*.

What makes this process remarkable is its ability to generate original, flowing text that appears to understand context and meaning. The model doesn't work from templates or pre-written responses—it constructs entirely *new content word by word*, with each decision influenced by the full context of what came before. This allows LLMs to generate everything from brief answers to lengthy essays, adapting their style and content as the text develops.

This idea that an LLM constructs its responses purely through the prediction of the next word is fundamental to understanding both its strengths and its limitations. This mechanism explains why LLMs can generate remarkably coherent text, but also why they can contradict themselves, lose track of context, or produce unexpected outputs. Keeping this principle in mind, we can now delve into the underlying mechanisms that drive this prediction process.

Assemble the Corpus

Building an LLM begins with assembling the **corpus**, the dataset on which the model is trained. Most of this data comes from web crawling, a process that systematically scans and collects content from the public internet. The corpus serves as the model's *foundational knowledge base*. But how exactly does this assembly process work?

Assembling the corpus involves several key steps (Figure 10.3). First, web crawlers collect text from millions of websites, creating a vast repository of written material. Since much of this content is repetitive, a deduplication process removes redundant text. The collected data is then formatted to ensure consistent and efficient processing. The final dataset often contains hundreds of billions or even *trillions* of words.

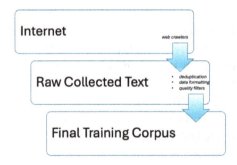

Figure 10.3: Corpus Assembly Pipeline. The process of building a training corpus for Large Language Models, from initial web crawling through deduplication and formatting to create the final training dataset.

The web-crawled data used to build large language models frequently comes from sources like **Common Crawl**, a non-profit project that regularly scans and archives vast portions of the Internet. Another widely used dataset is **Google's C4** (Colossal Clean Crawled Corpus)), which refines data from Common Crawl to improve quality, readability, and usefulness. These large-scale collections provide a diverse range of text from books, articles, forums, and other online sources.

Most large language models are trained on *multilingual* data, and many recent models are also *multi-modal*. Multi-modal models can process and generate not only text but also other forms of data such as images, audio, or video. While this book will not cover multi-modal architectures, the basic principles of language model training and functionality that we will explore apply similarly across these more complex systems. For simplicity, we will assume that the final dataset for our discussion is primarily in English. The end product can be conceptualized as a *single massive text file*, containing an extensive collection of written material that forms the basis for everything that follows in building the model.

It's important to recognize that a significant portion of publicly available data is problematic, containing misinformation, propaganda, bias, and harmful content such as misogyny and hate speech. Depending on the model, efforts are made to filter out low-quality or inappropriate material prior to training. However, for proprietary models, this filtering process is typically opaque, making it difficult to assess what content has been excluded and what biases may still remain in the final data set. This highlights a fundamental limitation: *an LLM on its own has no intrinsic ability to distinguish truth from falsehood, nor high-quality data from low-quality data.* The model learns patterns from whatever data it receives, making the quality and curation of the corpus critically important for the system's reliability and trustworthiness.

Define the Vocabulary

Once the corpus is assembled, the next step is to break the text into **tokens**, the fundamental building blocks of an LLM. A **token** can be a character, a word, a punctuation mark, or even part of a word. For example, the word *unhappiness* might be split into *un*, *happi*, and *ness*, recognizing common word components (Figure 10.4). This approach is more efficient than treating every word as a separate entity, which would require an impractically large vocabulary to account for all possible words.

LLMs use tokens instead of individual words for several key reasons:
- **Handling Multiple Languages and Word Variations**—Different languages have different word structures, and some writing systems do not use spaces between words. Tokenization allows models to process text more flexibly across

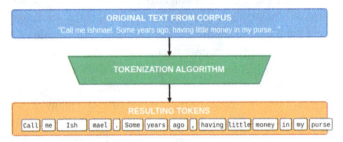

Figure 10.4: Text Tokenization Process. How text from Moby Dick is broken down into tokens during LLM preprocessing, showing the conversion from original text through tokenization algorithm to the resulting token sequence.

diverse writing systems by representing characters, subwords, or entire words as needed.

- **Efficiently Representing Rare and Complex Words**—Many words, especially technical terms, appear infrequently in training data. Instead of treating each as unique, tokenization breaks them into reusable subword units (e. g., *unhappiness* → [*un, happi, ness*]). This dramatically reduces vocabulary size while maintaining expressiveness.

- **Processing Unknown or New Words**—Language evolves constantly with new words, slang, and terminology. Tokenization allows the model to handle previously unseen words by breaking them into familiar components. For example, when encountering *bioprinting* for the first time, the model can still interpret it by splitting it into [*bio, printing*], leveraging its existing knowledge of these familiar components.

The collection of all unique tokens forms the **vocabulary** of an LLM, typically ranging from **50,000 to 100,000 tokens**. This fixed vocabulary represents the model's basic dictionary. The goal of tokenization is to create a compact yet expressive vocabulary capable of representing any text the model might encounter. This vocabulary serves as the crucial bridge between human language and the model's mathematical operations. Once text is tokenized, the next step is to transform these tokens into numerical representations—**embeddings**—that allow the model to learn the relationships between words.

Create Embeddings

This step is where the true *magic* of LLMs begins. Up until now, the model has processed text as a sequence of tokens—discrete symbols with no inherent meaning.

But machines cannot *understand* words the way humans do; they have no built-in intuition for the relationship between "king" and "queen," or the connection between "Paris" and "France." This critical step—**embedding**—is what *animates* these lifeless tokens, imbuing them with meaning. Through embedding, words transition from mere syntactical units to rich semantic entities with measurable relationships.

An embedding transforms each token into a high-dimensional vector—essentially a long list of numbers that acts as a unique mathematical fingerprint for that word or subword. Think of it as converting words into a special code that computers can work with (Figure 10.5).

TOKEN TO VECTOR EMBEDDING

High-dimensional vector

Figure 10.5: Token-to-Vector Conversion. An embedding transforms each token into a high-dimensional vector—a mathematical representation that captures semantic meaning and relationships.

To make this concept more concrete, imagine a simple coordinate system. On a two-dimensional map, for example, we can pinpoint a city using just two numbers: latitude and longitude. If we add more dimensions, we can capture additional information, such as elevation, climate, or population. Similarly, in the case of embeddings, instead of just two or three numbers, a word is represented by hundreds or even thousands of numbers, each encoding different aspects of its meaning. The result is a **semantic map of language**, where words with similar meanings cluster together, and relationships between concepts are expressed as properties of these many dimensions.

One of the most important goals of embedding is to position related words *closer* together in this mathematical space, so that words with similar meanings or that appear in similar contexts will have embeddings that place them near one another—just like how cities in the same region appear close together on a map.

In the simplified example shown in Figure 10.6, words with similar meanings cluster together. In the upper left quadrant, we see a group of sports-related terms: *baseball, basketball, soccer*. In the upper right, there's a cluster of fruit-related words: *strawberry, banana*, and *cherry*. Meanwhile, in the bottom left quadrant, we find technology companies such as *Google* and *Microsoft*.

Figure 10.6: Semantic Word Clustering. Two-dimensional visualization of word embeddings showing how related concepts naturally group together in vector space, with sports terms, fruits, and technology companies forming distinct clusters.

Of course, real embeddings go far beyond the two dimensions we can easily visualize—they operate in hundreds or even thousands of dimensions. This richer, higher-dimensional space allows the model to capture far more nuanced relationships between words. It's like going from a flat map to a complex model that can represent not just location but countless relationships between words—such as which words are masculine or feminine, which relate to science versus art, or which convey positive versus negative emotions.

This approach leads to interesting challenges. One challenge, for example, is: *where do we place ambiguous words?* Consider the word 'apple'. Should it be grouped with fruit or with technology companies?

A basic embedding (Figure 10.7) places 'apple' somewhere in between both clusters, reflecting its dual meaning. This demonstrates a fundamental limitation of simple embeddings: words with multiple meanings get *averaged out* into a single representation—a compromise that doesn't fully capture either meaning.

Fortunately, LLMs go beyond simple static embeddings. They use **context**—the surrounding words—to dynamically refine meaning. When the sentence mentions "Apple released a new iPhone," the model shifts or moves 'Apple' toward the technology cluster. When it reads "She ate a juicy apple," the model correctly associates it with fruit. We'll explore this mechanism in the next chapter. For now, understand that embeddings provide the initial **base vectors**, while later processing steps (covered in the next chapter) analyze surrounding words to resolve ambiguities and other subtle meanings.

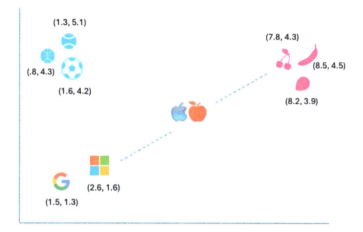

Figure 10.7: Visualization of how embeddings handle ambiguous words. The word 'apple' is positioned between the fruit cluster (upper right) and technology companies cluster (bottom left), illustrating how basic embeddings must compromise when representing words with multiple meanings. Icons for Apple Inc. and the fruit apple are shown in intermediate positions, demonstrating how a single vector representation struggles to capture distinct semantic meanings simultaneously.

In essence, embedding transforms words from simple symbols into *mathematical objects* that the model can dynamically adjust to build a rich semantics. It's like giving the computer a pair of special glasses that allow it to see not just the words themselves, but the invisible connections and relationships between them. This transformation is the foundation of everything that follows, allowing LLMs to capture subtle relationships and patterns that would be impossible with simplistic one-to-one mappings of words to meanings.

With our knowledge base assembled, our vocabulary defined, and our embeddings created, we now have the fundamental building blocks required to construct a language model. The raw text has been transformed into a structured format that machines can process, but the model has not yet learned how to use this information effectively. The next step, pre-training, is where the model will begin learning language patterns by predicting tokens in their proper context—much like how we learn language by predicting what word might come next in a sentence.

Pretrain Model Predictions

At its core, an LLM is a prediction enginee: it generates text by repeatedly predicting the next word. However, before it can generate meaningful responses, it must first learn language patterns. This learning happens during **pre-training**, a stage where the model trains itself on vast amounts of text by predicting words. Unlike traditional supervised learning, where humans provide explicit labels for each example, LLMs learn through **self-supervision**—the data itself provides the necessary signals for learning.

Understanding Self-Supervision

To understand the difference between supervised learning and self-supervision, let's consider a simple example:

In **supervised learning** (which we covered in previous chapters), a human must provide the correct answer for each example:

- Input: Image of a cat
- Human-provided label: "cat"
- The model learns to match or predict images consistent with human-provided labels

In **self-supervision**, the model creates its own learning examples from the raw data. Self-supervised learning in LLM pre-training typically follows one of two main approaches:

1. **Masked Language Modeling:** Random words in a sentence are masked (hidden), and the model must predict what the missing words should be. This allows learning from any position in the text.

2. **Next-Word Prediction:** The model sees the beginning of a sentence and must predict what comes next, one word at a time. This approach (also called autoregressive modeling) matches how LLMs will eventually be used.

Let's see how both approaches can generate training examples from a single sentence: 'The chef cooked a delicious meal'

Masked Language Modeling examples:

- **Input:** `___ chef cooked a delicious meal` → **Predict:** "The"
- **Input:** `The chef cooked a ___ meal` → **Predict:** "delicious"

Next-Word Prediction examples:

- **Input:** `The` → **Predict next word:** "chef"
- **Input:** `The chef` → **Predict next word:** "cooked"
- **Input:** `The chef cooked a delicious` → **Predict next word:** "meal"

Most modern LLMs are primarily trained using the next-word prediction approach, as this matches how they'll eventually be used—generating text one word at a time. However, some models use a combination of both approaches during pre-training.

To understand how pre-training works in practice, imagine teaching someone to solve puzzles. Instead of explaining each step, you simply give them thousands of incomplete puzzles and ask them to guess the missing piece. At first, they guess randomly. But over time, as they receive feedback on each attempt, they begin recognizing patterns—edge pieces belong on the borders, similar colors likely connect, and certain shapes fit together. Eventually, they become adept at predicting the right piece for any given gap.

This is precisely how an LLM learns. It is presented with billions of text fragments and is tasked with predicting words. For example:

- **Input:** The capital of France is
- **Task:** Predict the next word (*Paris*)
- **Input:** She
- **Task:** Predict the next word (*went, walked, drove, etc.*)
- **Input:** Mix the flour, sugar, and
- **Task:** Predict the next word (*eggs, butter, milk, etc.*)

Initially, the model makes many errors, but each incorrect prediction triggers an adjustment in its internal—billions of numerical values known as **weights**—to improve future guesses. It's like turning tiny knobs inside the model, each adjustment bringing it slightly closer to understanding language patterns.

Through this massive-scale pattern recognition, the model doesn't just memorize specific sentences—it learns general language rules, facts about the world, logical reasoning, and even some mathematical abilities, all without explicit instruction. Just as a child learns language patterns by hearing countless examples of speech, the model learns by processing text at a scale no human could ever achieve in a lifetime. This process is repeated trillions of times across the entire dataset—a scale of learning no human could achieve in multiple lifetimes.

From Prediction to Understanding

What makes this approach powerful is that, to predict words accurately, the model must internalize deep linguistic patterns. Without explicit instruction, it begins to develop:

- **Grammar and Syntax**—To predict the correct verb in a sentence, the model must learn sentence structure, subject-verb agreement, and the relationships between words.
- **World Knowledge**—To complete ``The capital of France is __.'', the model must recognize that *Paris* is the correct answer, acquiring factual associations through exposure to vast amounts of text.

- **Common Sense Reasoning**—To complete a phrase about baking a cake, the model must understand typical ingredients and human activities, distinguishing plausible completions from improbable ones.

This is an *emergent property* of scale: as the model encounters more text, it implicitly *discovers the rules of language* rather than being explicitly programmed with them. Much like a child immersed in language picks up grammatical structures before formally studying grammar, an LLM refines its understanding through exposure and prediction.

Shaping Model Behavior

After pre-training, a language model understands text in a statistical sense—it can predict words and generate grammatical sentences—but it lacks refinement in how it interacts with human. This is where **fine-tuning** comes in: the process that shapes the model's responses to be more coherent, contextually appropriate, and aligned with human expectations and values. Unlike pre-training, which focuses on general language patterns, fine-tuning adjusts the model's behavior to improve clarity, helpfulness, safety, and responsiveness in various types of interactions.

It's important to distinguish this type of fine-tuning from domain-specific training. While some researchers and practitioners use the term "fine-tuning" to refer to adding specialized knowledge to a model, here we focus specifically on the post-training adjustments that shape how the model interacts with humans, rather than expanding its knowledge base.

Think of pre-training as teaching someone vocabulary and grammar, while fine-tuning is more like teaching *social skills* and professional *etiquette*. The model already knows the language; now it needs to learn how to use it appropriately.

Learning from Human Examples

A key component of fine-tuning is supervised learning, where the model is trained on carefully curated examples that demonstrate preferred response styles. Human experts create these examples by writing sample user questions and crafting ideal responses that demonstrate desired qualities. These examples guide the model on when to be concise, when to elaborate, when to admit uncertainty, and how to maintain an appropriate tone. Through repeated exposure to thousands of high-quality responses, the model internalizes these stylistic and structural patterns, enhancing its adaptability across different conversational contexts.

Learning from Human Preferences

While supervised examples are valuable, they don't fully capture the nuanced preferences humans have about AI responses. To address this, models often undergo **reinforcement learning from human feedback (RLHF)**. This sophisticated approach works by having the model generate multiple possible responses to the same prompt, then having human reviewers rank these responses based on criteria such as helpfulness, accuracy, safety, and clarity. A reward model is trained to predict these human preferences, and the language model is then optimized to generate responses that would receive high ratings.

This iterative process reduces vague, misleading, or potentially harmful outputs while reinforcing responses that are clear, informative, and aligned with human values. It's like having thousands of people provide feedback on the model's work, helping it learn what humans actually prefer rather than just mimicking examples.

Real-World Impact

Fine-tuning transforms general-purpose language models into practical tools for specific applications. Consider customer service chatbots: without fine-tuning, a chatbot might provide technically correct but unhelpful answers like "I don't know" or overwhelm users with irrelevant technical details. After fine-tuning on support conversations, it learns to respond with the right level of detail, appropriate empathy, and clear next steps—becoming genuinely useful for customer support rather than just grammatically correct.

Fine-tuning ensures that LLMs don't just generate plausible-sounding text—they generate text that is useful, appropriate, safe, and aligned with users' needs. The model retains its broad knowledge but becomes more context-aware, more cautious when appropriate, and more effective in communication. While pre-training provides the fundamental capabilities, fine-tuning is what makes the model truly valuable as a tool for human use.

Conclusion

Throughout this chapter, we've traced the remarkable journey of how Large Language Models are constructed from raw internet text into sophisticated language generation systems capable of human-like conversation. This transformation happens through five fundamental steps, each building upon the previous ones to create something far greater than the sum of its parts.

We begin by assembling the corpus—gathering, cleaning, and organizing vast collections of text that serve as the model's knowledge foundation. This digital library provides the raw material from which the model learns language patterns, factual information, and cultural references. Next, we define the vocabulary by breaking text into tokens, creating the basic building blocks that allow models to handle any text they encounter, even unfamiliar words, by working with smaller, reusable components.

The third step, creating embeddings, transforms these tokens into high-dimensional mathematical representations that capture semantic relationships. This gives the model a way to understand not just individual words, but the invisible connections and relationships between concepts—allowing it to grasp similarities, differences, and contextual meanings that simple statistics couldn't achieve.

During pre-training, the model develops its fundamental language capabilities through billions of next-word predictions, gradually refining its internal representations until it can generate fluent, coherent text across virtually any topic. This self-supervised learning allows the model to discover language rules, factual associations, and reasoning patterns without explicit instruction.

Finally, through fine-tuning, we shape the model's raw capabilities into behavior that aligns with human preferences and expectations. This process teaches the model not just what it can say, but what it should say to be helpful, accurate, and safe—transforming a powerful but unpredictable system into a reliable assistant.

What emerges from this process is remarkable: a system that can discuss philosophy, explain scientific concepts, write creative stories, and help solve everyday problems. Yet understanding this construction reveals both the power and the limitations of these systems. They are sophisticated pattern-recognition engines trained on human-written text, capable of producing outputs that mirror human language capabilities, but they remain fundamentally statistical systems without true understanding of truth, accuracy, or real-world consequences.

As we'll see in the following chapters, addressing these limitations requires moving beyond pure language generation to systems that can verify information, cite sources, and take meaningful action in the world. The principles we've explored here—from tokens and embeddings to prediction and feedback—provide the foundation upon which these more advanced capabilities are built.

11 Foundation Models: How Large Language Models Become Smart

We propose a new simple network architecture, the Transformer, based solely on attention mechanisms, dispensing with recurrence and convolutions entirely.

—Ashish Vaswani et al.

The previous chapter explored how Large Language Models (LLMs) like ChatGPT are built from the ground up. Now, we shift our focus to how they actually function in real-time when responding to users. At the heart of modern LLMs is the **transformer architecture**, a breakthrough that has redefined artificial intelligence.

Earlier models struggled with language processing for two fundamental reasons. First, they processed text sequentially—word by word—making training prohibitively slow and expensive. Second, they often lost track of context over longer passages, severely limiting their understanding. Transformers overcame these limitations through two ground breaking innovations. They introduced parallel processing, analyzing entire sentences simultaneously rather than sequentially. They also developed the **attention mechanism**, which fundamentally transforms how machines understand language by dynamically modeling relationships between all words in a text. This mechanism allows the model to weigh the relevance of every word to every other word, creating a rich contextual understanding that captures nuance, resolves ambiguities, and maintains coherence across complex passages.

These innovations enable coherent and contextually aware responses at unprecedented scale. LLMs can now maintain consistency across long conversations and documents while processing information far more efficiently than previous approaches. By simultaneously addressing both speed and contextual awareness, transformers have unlocked the remarkable language capabilities we see in today's AI systems.

11.1 The Context Problem

A fundamental limitation of basic word embeddings is that they assign a fixed, static representation to each word, regardless of its meaning in context. For example, the word "apple" is mapped to a single fixed point in vector space, positioned somewhere between fruit and technology clusters.

This fixed positioning creates a fundamental challenge: if a word's location in vector space represents its meaning, how can we capture that "apple" could refer to either a fruit or a technology company—or countless other meanings? This ambiguity becomes a significant barrier since words frequently have multiple meanings

https://doi.org/10.1515/9783111583549-016

depending on their context. Human language is rich with such ambiguities—we routinely use the same words to mean different things and rely on surrounding context to clarify our intent.

Consider the different meanings of "apple" in everyday speech. It might refer to a fruit, the technology company that makes iPhones, or even serve as a metaphor in phrases like "apple of my eye." Our brains effortlessly distinguish between these meanings by examining the surrounding words. Traditional word embeddings, however, struggled with this fundamental aspect of language, as they had no mechanism to adjust word representations based on the specific context in which they appeared.

This context problem extends beyond simple word ambiguity. Understanding language requires tracking relationships between words across sentences, paragraphs, and entire books. It demands recognizing when different phrases refer to the same concept, grasping subtle shifts in topic, and maintaining coherence across long passages. Before transformers, AI systems lacked the architectural sophistication to effectively model these complex contextual relationships that humans navigate instinctively.

11.2 Context Windows: The Scope of Understanding

To solve the context problem, we must first understand how much information an AI system can process at once. This is where the concept of context windows becomes crucial. Just as humans have limited working memory, language models have constraints on how much text they can consider simultaneously.

A context window represents the maximum span of text an LLM can "see" and process at once. Think of it as the model's field of vision or working memory. When we interact with an LLM, it doesn't see the entire conversation history—it sees only as much as its context window allows (Figure 11.1).

Context windows determine several critical aspects of an LLM's capabilities. They control memory capacity, dictating how much previous conversation the model remembers. They define document processing limits, establishing the length of documents it can analyze at once. Perhaps most importantly, they shape reasoning scope, influencing the model's ability to connect information across long passages.

Early LLMs had limited context windows of perhaps a few hundred tokens, while modern models can process 100,000 tokens or more—equivalent to hundreds of pages of text. This dramatic expansion has fundamentally transformed what these systems can accomplish. In the foreseeable future, context windows of millions of tokens are likely to become mainstream.

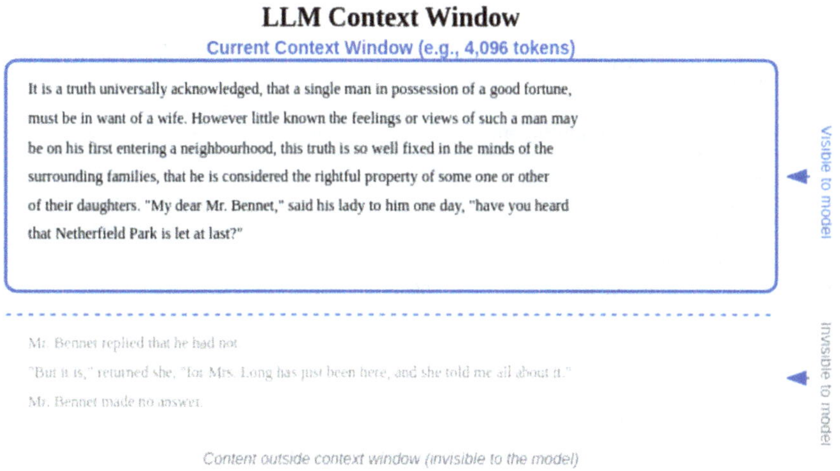

LLM Context Window

Current Context Window (e.g., 4,096 tokens)

It is a truth universally acknowledged, that a single man in possession of a good fortune, must be in want of a wife. However little known the feelings or views of such a man may be on his first entering a neighbourhood, this truth is so well fixed in the minds of the surrounding families, that he is considered the rightful property of some one or other of their daughters. "My dear Mr. Bennet," said his lady to him one day, "have you heard that Netherfield Park is let at last?"

visible to model

Mr. Bennet replied that he had not

"But it is," returned she, "for Mrs. Long has just been here, and she told me all about it."

Mr. Bennet made no answer.

invisible to model

Content outside context window (invisible to the model)

Figure 11.1: LLM Context Window as Working Memory. An LLM's context window functions as its working memory, determining how much text it can process simultaneously. While early models were limited to a few hundred tokens, modern architectures can process upwards of 100,000 tokens—equivalent to hundreds of pages of text—enabling more coherent reasoning across lengthy documents.

The context window is the playground where the attention mechanism operates. Within this window, every token can potentially attend to every other token. This is why expanding context windows has been a major focus of LLM development—it allows models to form more complex connections across longer texts, enabling them to maintain coherence over extended conversations or analyze comprehensive documents in their entirety.

However, larger context windows come with computational costs. Processing a 100,000-token context in real-time requires significantly more resources than processing a 2,000-token context. This tension between capability and efficiency drives much of the innovation in LLM architecture. Researchers continually seek methods to expand context while managing computational demands, developing clever approaches to make models more selective about what information they attend to or creating more efficient attention mechanisms that scale better to longer inputs. (See Table 11.1).

Understanding context windows helps explain both the capabilities and limitations of modern language models. When an LLM seems to "forget" something mentioned earlier in a conversation, struggles with a particularly lengthy document, or provides inconsistent responses, it's often bumping against the boundaries of its context window. Similarly, the remarkable improvements in coherence and reasoning we've seen in recent years stem largely from the expansion of these windows, allowing models to maintain and integrate more information simultaneously.

Table 11.1: Evolution of Context Window Sizes. The dramatic expansion of context windows in large language models from 2021 to 2025, showing the progression from thousands to hundreds of thousands of tokens.

Year	Model (Company/Organization)	Context Window Size (Tokens)
2021	GPT-3 (OpenAI)	4,000
2022	PaLM (Google)	8,000
2023	LLaMA 2 (Meta)	32,000
2024	Claude-X (Anthropic)	100,000+
2024	Gemini 1.5 Pro (Google)	128,000 (Standard), up to 2 million (Extended)
2025	Claude 3.7 Sonnet (Anthropic)	200,000

11.3 Transformer Architecture

Now that we understand the context problem and the scope of what transformers can "see," let's examine how the transformer architecture addresses these challenges.

A transformer consists of multiple layers stacked on top of each other, with each layer progressively refining the model's understanding of language in a step-by-step process. Think of each layer as a specialized lens that focuses on different aspects of language, with the entire stack working together to build a comprehensive understanding (Figure 11.2).

Figure 11.2: Basic Transformer Layer Architecture. Input text passes through an attention block that establishes contextual relationships between words, followed by a feed-forward block that processes each word's representation independently.

Each layer in the stack is built from two essential components:

1. **Attention Layer**—This component determines how words influence one another within a sentence. Transformers analyze all words simultaneously, dynamically adjusting their importance based on context. This parallel approach captures relationships across long passages, ensuring a nuanced understanding of text.

2. **Feed-Forward Layer**—Once the attention layer has established contextual re-lationships, the feed-forward layer enhances each word's representation inde-pendently. It applies transformations that refine meaning, filter out noise, and extract deeper linguistic patterns.

These layers are repeated multiple times, forming a deep stack. Underneath the hood is a deep learning neural network of the kind we saw in previous chapters. Modern LLMs contain dozens of these layers, enabling them to process complex concepts with remarkable accuracy and nuance. Each successive layer builds upon the work of previous layers, gradually transforming raw text input into rich, con-textual representations that capture the subtle nuances of language (Figure 11.3).

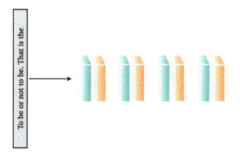

Figure 11.3: Multi-Layer Transformer Architecture. Text representations flow through repeated attention and feed-forward blocks, with each layer progressively refining contextual understanding and extracting deeper linguistic patterns.

The genius of this architecture lies in its ability to simultaneously consider both local and global context. While traditional approaches might only focus on nearby words, transformers can weigh the importance of every word relative to every other word in the passage. This comprehensive approach allows them to resolve ambigu-ities, track references across long distances, and maintain coherence throughout extended texts.

As information flows through this layered structure, the model develops an in-creasingly sophisticated understanding of the input text. Early layers might capture basic syntactic relationships, while deeper layers develop more abstract semantic representations. By the final layer, the model has constructed a rich internal rep-resentation that can be used to generate appropriate responses, complete tasks, or answer questions with remarkable fluency and accuracy.

11.4 The Attention Mechanism

Let's now work through an example to see how the attention mechanism resolves ambiguity. Suppose we are given the following sentence:

> "The woman went to the bank adjacent to the river bank to deposit her money. Meanwhile, she was also thinking about practicing bank shots for her upcoming basketball game."

The word "bank" appears three times, each with a completely different meaning:
1. A financial institution
2. The side of a river
3. A basketball shot technique

With basic word embeddings, all three instances of "bank" are assigned the same vector representation. The solution to resolving the ambiguity begins with positional encoding, followed by the attention mechanism.

11.4.1 Positional Encoding

Before the attention mechanism begins its work, the model combines each word's base embedding with its position in the sentence. This ensures that the model can differentiate between multiple occurrences of the same word.

Although all three instances of "bank" start with the same base embedding, each instance is tagged with different positional information:

> "The woman went to the [$bank_1$] adjacent to the river [$bank_2$] to deposit her money. Meanwhile, she was also thinking about practicing [$bank_3$] shots for her upcoming basketball game."

In the sentence above, [$bank_1$], [$bank_2$], and [$bank_3$] represent the new embedding with the positional encoding inserted. This now allows us to distinguish and independently track the three separate instances of the word "bank".

It's important to understand that the basic embedding for each token in the vocabulary is created during pre-training and remains fixed. However, when a user interacts with an LLM, each embedding is dynamically updated to capture each token's particular semantics in that specific context. This dynamic updating is precisely what allows the model to resolve ambiguity.

We are now ready to understand the operations performed by the attention block, the transformer component which determines relationships between words, ensuring that each word shifts in meaning based on surrounding context.

11.4.2 Visualizing the Attention Mechanism

To visualize the attention mechanism, imagine words as celestial bodies floating in space. When a new sentence enters the model, the attention mechanism acts like a gravitational field, continuously pushing and pulling each word based on its context towards its correct semantic position.

The process works in three key steps:

1. **Initial Embedding:** We saw in the last chapter that each token is mapped to a base embedding vector, its starting representation in vector space.

2. **Positional Encoding:** Next, the model adds positional information to indicate where each token appears in the sequence. This step also allows the model to track each occurrence of ambiguous words separately.

3. **Dynamic Adjustment:** As the model processes the text in the attention block, the attention mechanism updates each token's representation based on its relationships with other tokens:
    -   For $bank_1$ (Financial Institution), words like "deposit" and "money" exert a stronger influence, pulling it toward financial meanings.
    -   For $bank_2$ (Geographical Feature), "river" exerts the strongest pull, shifting its meaning toward geographical terms.
    -   For $bank_3$ (Basketball Shot), "shots" and "basketball game" align it with sports-related meanings.

By the time the attention block has processed the sentence, the three instances of "bank" have dynamically adjusted their vector representations to reflect their specific contextual meanings. In a typical transformer architecture, the sentence moves through multiple attention blocks and the calibration of the embeddings becomes increasingly more accurate (Figure 11.4).

11.5 Vector Dimensions: Beyond Position in Space

So far, we've described embedding vectors primarily in terms of their position in vector space—where a word sits relative to other words. This is useful but incomplete. Embedding vectors aren't just points in space; they're arrows with both magnitude and direction and each dimension of these vectors encodes meaningful semantic properties.

Modern embedding spaces typically have hundreds or thousands of dimensions—far more than we can visualize. Each dimension captures some aspect of meaning. While individual dimensions rarely correspond to single interpretable concepts, certain directions in the embedding space represent meaningful semantic relationships.

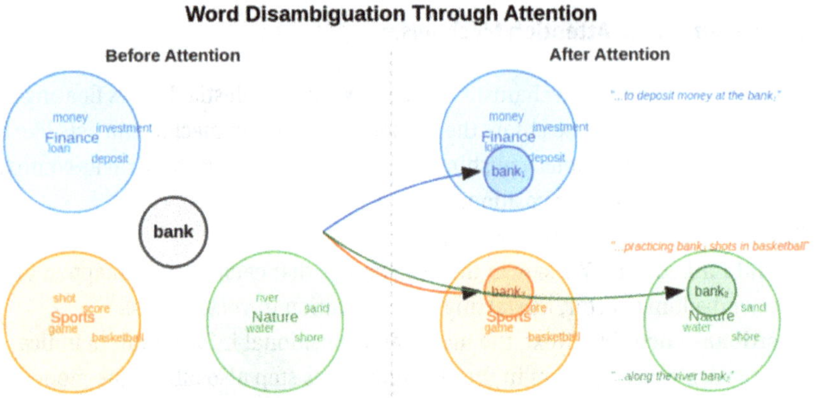

Figure 11.4: Dynamic Word Disambiguation Through Attention. The attention mechanism moves ambiguous instances of "bank" from an initial shared representation (left) to appropriate semantic clusters based on context (right).

One of the most fascinating properties of word embeddings is that we can perform arithmetic on them to reveal semantic relationships. The classic example is:

$$king - man + woman \approx queen \tag{11.1}$$

This equation suggests that the vector difference between "king" and "man" captures something like "royalty" or "leadership," while the difference between "man" and "woman" captures gender. By combining these relationships, we can navigate the embedding space in semantically meaningful ways (Figure 11.5).

Researchers have identified many semantic directions in embedding spaces:
- Paris – France + Italy ≈ Rome (capital-country relationship)
- good – bad ≈ pleasant – unpleasant (sentiment direction)
- walking – walked ≈ running – ran (tense direction)

The attention mechanism doesn't just shift words' positions; it recalculates the entire vector, adjusting each dimension to better reflect contextual meaning. This allows LLMs to capture nuanced semantic properties that go beyond simple word similarity.

For instance, when processing "I need to deposit money at the bank," the attention mechanism strengthens dimensions associated with financial transactions while dampening dimensions related to natural geography or sports. This multidimensional adjustment ensures that when the model encounters "bank" in this context, the word's representation emphasizes its financial meaning across all relevant dimensions.

These nuanced adjustments happen across thousands of dimensions simultaneously, allowing the model to capture subtle semantic distinctions that would be

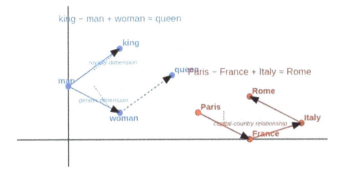

Figure 11.5: Semantic Relationships in Word Embedding Space. Vector arithmetic reveals meaningful patterns, such as analogies (king − man + woman ≈ queen) and consistent relationships (Paris − France + Italy ≈ Rome). Note that this 2D visualization is a simplified representation of actual embedding vectors, which have hundreds or thousands of dimensions, each capturing different semantic properties.

impossible with simpler approaches. While we may visualize embedding space in two or three dimensions for simplicity, it's important to remember that the true power of these representations comes from their high-dimensional nature, where each dimension contributes to the rich tapestry of meaning that language models can understand.

11.6 Feed-Forward Layer

While the attention mechanism ensures that words are positioned correctly in context, the feed-forward layer plays a different role—it optimizes each word's internal structure to ensure clarity and efficiency.

Think of this process as similar to a solar panel optimization system. Angle optimization adjusts each word's representation, amplifying relevant features and discarding irrelevant information. Cleaning and maintenance filters out noise or weak influences picked up during the attention phase. Energy conversion applies transformations that refine meaning for the next processing layers.

The attention mechanism establishes the correct contextual positioning for each word—like gravity shaping planetary orbits. The feed-forward layer refines each word's internal representation—like a solar panel maximizing energy absorption. Together, they construct meaning dynamically with both precision and efficiency.

The feed-forward component consists of neural networks that process each word individually. Unlike the attention mechanism, which connects words across the entire context, these networks focus solely on enhancing individual word representations. This separation of concerns is crucial: attention determines relationships between words, while feed-forward networks enrich those words based on the relationships that have been established.

Technically, these feed-forward networks are simple yet powerful. Each one typically contains two linear transformations with a non-linear activation function in between. This structure allows the model to learn complex patterns about how contextual information should reshape word representations.

For example, after the attention mechanism has connected our financial "bank" with words like "deposit" and "money," the feed-forward layer processes this enriched representation. It might amplify dimensions related to financial services while suppressing irrelevant features, resulting in a cleaner, more focused representation that better captures the intended meaning in that specific context.

By alternating between attention and feed-forward layers throughout the transformer stack, the model gradually refines its understanding of each word's meaning in context. This complementary process ensures both relationship awareness and representation clarity, providing the foundation for the remarkable language capabilities we observe in modern LLMs.

11.7 Attention Beyond Ambiguity

The attention mechanism does more than resolve word ambiguity. It tracks meaning across long passages, prioritizes important words, and refines language understanding at each stage of processing.

One powerful feature of attention is connecting words that are far apart in text. Consider:

> "After she graduated from medical school in Boston, which took eight challenging years, Dr. Chen decided to practice in her hometown."

A human reader easily understands that "she" refers to Dr. Chen, despite the distance between them. The attention mechanism enables this connection by allowing words to "attend to" relevant words regardless of distance.

In traditional sequence models, this connection would be difficult to maintain as information would need to pass through many intermediate steps. The attention mechanism creates a direct path between these words, preserving the relationship even across long distances.

Not every word carries equal importance. The attention mechanism helps LLMs prioritize key words by assigning weights indicating relevance. In the question "What year was the Eiffel Tower completed?", attention identifies "year," "Eiffel Tower," and "completed" as most relevant, while giving minimal weight to function words like "the" and "was."

This selective focus is essential for answering questions, summarizing documents, and generating on-topic responses. By concentrating computational resources on the most meaningful parts of text, the model can more effectively capture the core meaning of a passage.

The weighting process is dynamic and contextual—the same word might receive high attention in one context and low attention in another. This adaptability allows LLMs to focus on what matters in each specific situation, mimicking how humans naturally emphasize certain parts of language during comprehension.

11.8 Putting It All Together: A Complete Example

Let's walk through how an LLM processes the prompt: "What are some famous landmarks in Paris?"

Step 1: Tokenization

The model breaks the input into tokens:

```
["What", "are", "some", "famous", "landmarks", "in", "Paris", "?"]
```

Step 2: Initial Embedding and Positional Encoding

Each token receives an initial embedding vector and positional information. The embedding represents the basic meaning of the word, while the positional encoding captures where each token appears in the sequence. This combination allows the model to differentiate between the same word appearing in different positions and helps maintain awareness of word order.

Step 3: Processing Through Transformer Layers

- **Attention Mechanism:** "landmarks" begins interacting with "Paris," which pulls "landmarks" toward Parisian-specific locations. Similarly, "What" interacts strongly with "landmarks" and "Paris" as these tokens are crucial for answering the question.
- **Feed-Forward Processing:** The feed-forward layer refines each token individually, strengthening contextual associations while filtering out irrelevant connections. The token representation for "landmarks" becomes more specifically oriented toward famous structures rather than generic landmarks.
- **Deeper Layers:** As processing continues through multiple transformer layers, "landmarks" shifts toward specific Parisian locations, and the model activates knowledge about these landmarks. Each layer progressively refines the representation, with earlier layers capturing syntax and basic semantics while deeper layers develop more nuanced conceptual understanding.

Step 4: Response Generation

The model generates a response one token at a time:

"Some of the most famous landmarks in Paris include the Eiffel Tower, the Louvre Museum, and Notre-Dame Cathedral..."

With each new word, the model reprocesses the sequence, maintaining coherence and relevance through the attention mechanism. The previously generated tokens become part of the context window, influencing the selection of subsequent tokens. The model continues this process, leveraging its understanding of Parisian landmarks to produce a coherent, informative response.

Throughout this entire process, each layer of the transformer architecture contributes to building a coherent understanding, from initial word representations to contextual relationships to the final generated text.

11.9 Conclusion

The journey through transformer architecture reveals how Large Language Models process text in real-time, transforming raw input into meaningful, contextually rich responses.

The attention mechanism stands as the cornerstone of this architecture, resolving ambiguity by allowing words to dynamically influence each other based on context. It strengthens long-distance relationships across text, ensuring that relevant connections remain intact regardless of separation. Furthermore, it intelligently prioritizes important words, focusing computational resources where they matter most.

Complementing this, feed-forward layers refine individual word representations, filtering noise and reinforcing patterns that enhance overall understanding. This combination of broad contextual awareness and focused refinement creates the foundation for language models' remarkable capabilities.

The power of transformers lies in their ability to adapt and generalize. By continuously updating word representations at every stage, they recognize complex relationships, understand nuanced queries, and generate responses aligned with user intent. This adaptability extends beyond simple word substitution to encompass sophisticated reasoning about concepts, relationships, and implications.

The transformer architecture represents a fundamental shift in how machines process language. Rather than viewing text as a linear sequence of fixed-meaning words, transformers model language as a dynamic web of interconnected concepts, where meaning emerges from the complex interplay between words in context. This perspective aligns more closely with how humans understand language, explaining why modern LLMs exhibit such remarkable linguistic capabilities.

Understanding how these models function is essential to grasping their strengths, limitations, and potential future advancements in artificial intelligence. As we continue to refine and expand this architecture, we move closer to systems that can not only process language but truly understand it in all its rich complexity.

12 Expert Models: Grounding AI in Trusted Knowledge

A lot of it is a matter of stating the obvious-but stating the obvious is not always easy when one begins with a confused domain.

—Harry Collins

In earlier chapters, we explored the inner workings of Foundation Models and how they have revolutionized AI, enabling machines to tackle tasks once thought impossible. Yet despite their power, these models have significant limitations: they can falter in reliability, accuracy, and practical application.

This is where **Expert Models**, or **Retrieval-Augmented Generation (RAG)** systems, come in. Rather than replacing Foundation Models, they build on them—connecting to *external sources of knowledge* to overcome key weaknesses while preserving the strengths of language generation.

We begin with a *visual comparison* of the two approaches to build intuition around how they differ. Then we dive into the *limitations* of Foundation Models—why even the most advanced systems struggle with historical accuracy, factual grounding, and verifiability.

Next, we walk through a *real-world example*: a nurse seeking medical guidance in a clinical setting. We then examine how Expert Models *work*, showing how retrieval and augmentation with trusted sources improve performance and reliability.

Finally, we turn to *design considerations and trade-offs*. While Expert Models offer a powerful solution, realizing their potential requires care. These systems are not plug-and-play. Their reliability, interpretability, and adaptability hinge on design choices—some technical, others organizational—all involving trade-offs. We conclude by examining three key design factors: the quality of the knowledge base, the nature of expert knowledge, and the importance of source provenance.

12.1 Comparing Approaches—Foundation vs. Expert Models

Before diving into the mechanics of how Expert Models work, let's begin with a side-by-side look at how they differ from traditional Foundation Models. A visual comparison offers a helpful starting point for building intuition about what sets these two approaches apart.

https://doi.org/10.1515/9783111583549-017

Foundation Model Approach

In the Foundation Model approach (Figure 12.1), a user interacts directly with a Large Language Model (LLM) by posing a query or prompt. The process works as follows:

1. The user submits a question or request.
2. The LLM processes this input using only its pre-trained knowledge.
3. The model generates a response based solely on patterns it learned during training.
4. The response is returned to the user without validation from external sources.

While this approach allows for fluent and coherent answers across a wide range of topics, the model is inherently constrained by the knowledge it acquired during training. It cannot incorporate new information, verify its claims against current sources, or acknowledge when it lacks sufficient knowledge.

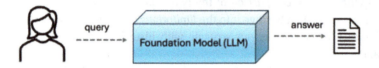

Figure 12.1: Foundation Model-only approach. The user queries the LLM, which generates a response based only on its pre-trained knowledge.

Expert Model Approach

In contrast, the Expert Model approach (Figure 12.2) introduces a critical enhancement: access to external knowledge. The process works as follows:

1. The user submits a question or request.
2. A retrieval component analyzes the query to determine what information is needed.
3. The retriever searches through specialized databases, trusted documents, or knowledge bases to find relevant information.
4. The retrieved information is combined with the original query.
5. The Foundation Model processes both the query and the retrieved information.
6. The model generates a response that integrates both its inherent language capabilities and the specific retrieved knowledge.
7. The response, often including citations to the sources used, is returned to the user.

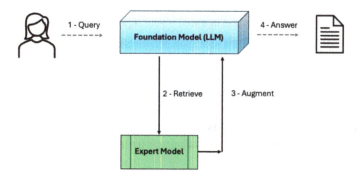

Figure 12.2: Expert Model/RAG approach. The LLM consults external knowledge sources via a retriever, integrating specialized knowledge into its response.

This mechanism ensures that, at least in theory, answers are informed by verifiable, potentially current knowledge while retaining the language fluency of the Foundation Model. The key difference is that Expert Models don't just rely on what they "learned" during training—they actively seek out specialized knowledge to inform their responses. This fundamentally changes their relationship with information, enabling them to cite sources, access up-to-date facts, and respond with greater reliability.

12.2 The Limitations of Foundation Models

The visual comparison above highlights a key distinction: Foundation Models generate responses based solely on what they learned during training, while Expert Models may consult external knowledge in real time. But what, exactly, are the consequences of relying on pre-trained knowledge alone?

Despite their remarkable abilities, Foundation Models face serious limitations that affect their reliability and practical use. They struggle to stay current, often produce plausible but incorrect information, cannot cite their sources, and may respond inconsistently to the same query. Let's examine each of these limitations in turn.

The Knowledge Cutoff Problem

Even with their extensive general knowledge, Foundation Models operate with a fixed knowledge base that ends at a specific training cutoff date. No matter how comprehensive the data they were trained on, they cannot access information that emerged afterward.

This is like using an encyclopedia last updated a year ago. It may be rich in information but silent on recent discoveries, events, or shifts in public understanding. The problem is especially acute in fast-moving domains like medicine, science, or global affairs. A model trained in early 2024, for example, would have no awareness of events or developments that occurred after that point.

To make matters worse, Foundation Models often do not disclose this limitation. When asked about post-cutoff topics, they typically generate answers as if they are up to date, offering no indication that their knowledge is frozen in time.

The Hallucination Challenge

A second issue is hallucination—the generation of confident but false or fabricated information.

As we have seen, Foundation Models do not retrieve facts from a validated database. Instead, they predict the next most likely word in a sequence based on statistical patterns in their training data. When the model lacks certainty, it may still offer an answer that sounds authoritative, even if it's completely made up. This is why models sometimes cite nonexistent research papers, describe fictional events as real, or provide incorrect but precisely stated details (Rawte et al., 2023).

This can have serious real-world consequences. In academic research, fabricated citations have appeared in published work. In healthcare, AI-generated medical advice has included inaccurate or harmful suggestions. In law, attorneys have submitted briefs citing imaginary court cases. The problem isn't just that Foundation Models make mistakes—it's that they make them with persuasive conviction.

The Provenance Problem

Even when a Foundation Model gives a correct answer, it cannot explain where the information came from. Ask, "Where did you get this?"—and the model has no way to respond meaningfully. It cannot cite its sources, trace its reasoning, or validate the facts it presents.

This lack of provenance is a serious trust issue. In domains like science, journalism, medicine, or law, being able to verify the source of a claim is essential. Without that traceability, users have no way to assess the reliability of what the model says.

And it's not just about citation—it's about transparency. Foundation Models generate responses based on hidden probabilities. They don't show their work in a way humans can understand. That makes it hard for users to tell whether an answer is grounded in something trustworthy or simply a byproduct of pattern prediction.

The Inconsistency Problem

Another weakness of Foundation Models is their inconsistency. Unlike traditional software, which produces the same output for the same input, language models can give different answers to the same question, even seconds apart.

Imagine visiting a doctor with a specific set of symptoms. You're diagnosed with strep throat. One hour later, you return with the same symptoms—and now you're told it's allergies. That would shake your confidence in the diagnosis. Yet this is common behavior for Foundation Models.

Why? Because they are probabilistic systems. Each response is generated by sampling from a distribution of likely next words. This randomness means that small differences—or even none at all—can lead to different outputs.

Deterministic systems provide the same output every time they receive identical inputs—like traditional software or the classification models we explored earlier. When you ask a deterministic calculator what 2 + 2 equals, you'll always get 4. Stochastic systems involve an element of randomness or probability. Given the same input, they may produce different outputs each time—like Foundation Models. This is why asking the same question twice might yield two different answers.

This distinction has crucial implications: In fields like healthcare, finance, or law, inconsistent advice can be dangerous. Users need to trust that recommendations won't change arbitrarily. Inconsistent outputs make it difficult to verify system behavior through testing. How do you know if a system is working correctly if it changes its mind each time? Inconsistency confuses users and erodes trust. Imagine if your GPS recalculated the "fastest route" every minute, giving different directions each time. Most programming environments, tools, and testing frameworks are built around the assumption of determinism. Debugging, quality assurance, and continuous integration become significantly more complex when outputs can vary without changes to inputs.

This variability is more than an annoyance. In fields where consistency matters—like healthcare, law, education, and business—it undermines trust. Even when tuned to be more deterministic (by setting the model's "temperature" to zero), subtle differences in reasoning or detail may persist, especially with complex or ambiguous.

The deeper paradox is this: the more important and nuanced the question, the more likely it is that the model's answer will vary or fall short.

The Limits of Scale

It's tempting to think that these problems can be solved simply by scaling up—training larger models, more often, on more data. But this approach runs into hard limits.

Training massive models is computationally expensive, and even frequent re-training can't eliminate the lag between real-world events and model knowledge. More importantly, size does not equal truth. A bigger model may be more fluent, but just as likely to be wrong.

That's because Foundation Models don't understand truth. They don't "know" facts—they learn patterns. Making them bigger doesn't give them the ability to verify claims or distinguish between fact and fiction. Without an external grounding mechanism, they remain powerful but untrustworthy tools.

Why Expert Models Are Needed

These inherent limitations—outdated knowledge, hallucinations, lack of provenance, inconsistency, and the limits of scaling—reveal the boundaries of what Foundation Models can do on their own. Foundation Models excel at statistical prediction, but are not reliable knowledge systems.

Addressing these challenges requires a new approach—one that supplements language generation with external, verifiable sources of information. That's the promise of Expert Models. In the next section, we explore how these systems work and why they represent a critical step forward in building more trustworthy AI.

12.3 Applied Example: Medical Guidance in Clinical Settings

To see how these different approaches play out in real-world situations, consider a scenario in healthcare—where accuracy, consistency, and up-to-date information can have a direct impact on patient outcomes. Imagine a nurse at Riverside Medical Center (fictitious) seeking guidance on a specialized medical question:

> **Nurse:** What are the latest treatment guidelines for managing atrial fibrillation in elderly patients with chronic kidney disease?

Let's compare how a Foundation Model and an Expert Model might respond and what these differences reveal about their capabilities.

Standard AI Response (Foundation Model)

A Foundation Model, working without access to current medical literature or institutional protocols, might respond with something like this:

> **AI Medical Assistant:** Atrial fibrillation (AF) in elderly patients with chronic kidney disease (CKD) is typically managed with anticoagulation therapy to reduce stroke risk. Warfarin has traditionally been used, but newer direct oral anticoagulants (DOACs) are often preferred due to their ease of use. However, patients with CKD, especially those with advanced stages, require careful monitoring for bleeding risks. In general, treatment decisions should balance stroke prevention with bleeding risk, and renal function should be regularly assessed.

While this response is coherent and medically plausible, it reveals several limitations. It offers general rather than specific guidance, lacks citations or references to current guidelines, omits hospital-specific protocols, and provides no indication of how up-to-date the information is.

Worse, if the nurse were to ask the same question again later, the model might produce a different—perhaps even contradictory—answer. One version might emphasize anticoagulation, while another might suggest rate control strategies, despite no change in the evidence or the patient's condition. In healthcare, this kind of inconsistency can undermine trust and compromise care.

Though not necessarily incorrect, the information reads more like content from a medical textbook than a reliable source of clinical decision support. Without context, currency, or consistency, its practical value is limited. It can also be dangerous.

Enhanced AI Response (Expert Model)

Now consider the same query processed by an Expert Model equipped with access to up-to-date clinical guidelines and institutional policies. The response might look like this:

> **AI Medical Assistant:** According to the 2023 guidelines from the American College of Cardiology (ACC) and the European Society of Cardiology (ESC), the management of atrial fibrillation in elderly patients with chronic kidney disease (CKD) requires a tailored approach based on renal function. [citation link] For patients with CKD stage 3 (eGFR 30–59 mL/min), DOACs such as apixaban or edoxaban are preferred over warfarin due to their lower risk of major bleeding. However, in patients with CKD stage 4 (eGFR 15–29 mL/min), dose adjustments are necessary, and warfarin may still be considered. For those with end-stage renal disease (CKD stage 5), recent studies suggest apixaban may be safer than warfarin, but this remains an area of ongoing research. [citation links] Before prescribing anticoagulation, clinicians should consult updated renal dosing guidelines and consider patient-specific bleeding risks. For more details, see the 2023 ACC guideline update here: [citation link].

> Additionally, at Riverside Medical Center, hospital protocols require that no anticoagulation therapy be initiated or adjusted for CKD patients with atrial fibrillation without prior consultation with the Cardiorenal Specialty Team. Clinicians must coordinate with the Cardiorenal Consultation Unit (CCU) before proceeding with treatment to ensure adherence to the latest institutional guidelines and best practices. [citation link]

This response demonstrates the strengths of the Expert Model. It references specific, current clinical guidelines; provides tailored recommendations based on disease stage; includes citations to trusted sources; and incorporates institution-specific procedures—all within the context of the nurse's original question.

Importantly, the response should be consistent across multiple queries—as long as the underlying guidelines remain unchanged. That consistency is essential in clinical environments, where decisions must follow established, evidence-based protocols. By grounding its output in specific, retrievable sources, the Expert Model avoids the variability that plagues Foundation Models and builds the kind of trust required for high-stakes decision-making.

Why This Matters

This example illustrates how the differences between Foundation and Expert Models aren't just theoretical—they have real implications for usability, safety, and trust.

The Expert Model doesn't merely sound more authoritative; it is more grounded and useful. It delivers information that is current, verifiable, context-aware, and institutionally aligned. It tells users where its information came from, making it easier to assess reliability and act on the guidance with confidence.

This distinction becomes even more critical in rapidly evolving domains or when decisions must be made based on the latest available evidence. Both systems can generate fluent language—but only one can reliably deliver information grounded in authoritative sources.

As shown in Table 12.1, Expert Models address the core limitations of Foundation Models by combining retrieval with generation:

Table 12.1: How RAG addresses Foundation Model limitations.

Foundation Model Limitation	RAG Solution
Knowledge Cutoff	Access to updatable knowledge sources
Hallucination	Grounding in retrieved factual content
Lack of Provenance	Ability to cite specific sources
Inconsistency	Stable answers from consistent inputs
Scaling Constraints	Domain expertise without massive model size

In domains where accuracy, consistency, and verifiability are not optional, Expert Models offer a path forward. With this foundation, let's now explore how these systems are designed—and the trade-offs involved in building them well.

12.4 How Expert Models Work

Expert Models represent a significant evolution in how AI systems process and respond to user inputs. While the basic idea—retrieving information before generating a response—may seem simple, the underlying architecture and design choices are complex and consequential. These choices shape a system's reliability, trustworthiness, and practical value.

Core Architecture and Workflow

At the heart of an Expert Model is a system of interconnected components. The user's query initiates the process. First, the system analyzes the question to determine what kind of information is needed. Then, a retrieval component searches a curated knowledge store—an external repository of trusted content—and selects relevant material. This information is combined with the original query and passed to a Foundation Model, which generates a response grounded in both language fluency and factual relevance (Lewis et al., 2020).

This process may sound straightforward, but what makes it powerful is its modular design. The knowledge store can be updated independently of the Foundation Model, allowing organizations to keep information current without retraining the entire system. This modularity makes Expert Models adaptable and scalable, particularly in fields where knowledge evolves quickly (IBM Research, 2024).

Importantly, the sources of expertise accessed during retrieval are not limited to a single repository. Depending on the use case, an Expert Model might consult internal databases, domain-specific resources, live data feeds, or even smaller expert-trained models that specialize in particular subject areas. This flexibility enables customization to the needs of healthcare providers, legal professionals, educators, or business users.

Understanding External Knowledge

Expert Models draw on a variety of external knowledge sources, each with distinct roles in supporting system performance.

Some of the most essential are authoritative knowledge bases—such as clinical guidelines or legal codes—that provide well-defined, high-trust information for specific fields. These sources are often curated by professional organizations or regulatory bodies and serve as foundational references.

In contrast, organizational knowledge includes internal materials specific to a particular institution. These might consist of policies, procedures, proprietary data, or institutional protocols. Integrating this knowledge allows the system to respond with guidance that reflects local practices or company-specific rules.

Another source of external knowledge comes in the form of specialized language models—so-called expert LLMs—that are fine-tuned on domain-specific data. These models can be queried within the broader system to provide detailed or technical responses in areas such as law, finance, or medicine.

Finally, real-time data feeds address the limitations of static training by supplying up-to-date information. These might include APIs for financial markets, weather conditions, or news updates. In fast-changing environments, access to current data is essential to maintain relevance.

From Retrieval to Reasoning: The Integration Challenge

Retrieving knowledge is only the first step. The real challenge lies in how that information is integrated into the model's final response. At a basic level, the system appends retrieved text to the user's query and sends this combined prompt to the Foundation Model. However, more sophisticated systems apply additional logic during this step.

For example, they may prioritize more reliable sources over others, resolve conflicts when retrieved content contains contradictory claims, or flag uncertainty when information is incomplete. The system may also adjust how much retrieved content to include based on the complexity of the query. All of these decisions affect not only what the model says, but how confident users can be in its responses.

Another key consideration is transparency. Some systems instruct the model to cite its sources directly or include links to relevant documents. This allows users to trace the origins of a response and evaluate its credibility for themselves—an essential feature in domains where accountability matters.

What Makes a Model an "Expert"?

Not every system that retrieves external information qualifies as an Expert Model. The difference lies in how knowledge is selected, verified, and integrated. A chatbot that pulls content indiscriminately from the internet may technically use retrieval, but it lacks the safeguards and precision associated with true expertise.

Expert Models are defined by their intentionality. They draw from sources that have been vetted for accuracy. They provide transparency about where information comes from. And they are designed to deliver responses that are both contextually appropriate and grounded in trustworthy knowledge.

In practice, this means Expert Models are carefully engineered—not only to retrieve relevant facts, but also to represent uncertainty when appropriate, resolve ambiguity when possible, and adapt to the specific needs of users in high-stakes environments.

Retrieval and Updating: A Strategic Advantage

A key advantage of Expert Models is their ability to separate the knowledge base from the language generation model. Unlike traditional Foundation Models, which require retraining to incorporate new knowledge, Expert Models can update their knowledge store independently. This enables them to respond to new developments without overhauling the entire system.

Behind the scenes, the knowledge store is preprocessed into smaller text chunks and transformed into vector embeddings—mathematical representations that capture semantic meaning. When a user submits a query, it too is converted into a vector, and the system uses similarity metrics to identify the most relevant chunks of content. This allows the system to match meaning, not just keywords, and surface information that may be expressed in different terms.

The effectiveness of this approach depends on the depth and quality of the knowledge store, as well as the system's ability to interpret queries accurately. Gaps in coverage or ambiguity in user input can lead to incomplete or misleading responses. That's why continuous refinement—both of the knowledge base and the retrieval process—is critical for Expert Model performance.

Balancing Fluency and Fidelity

The final response generated by an Expert Model reflects a balance between fluency and fidelity. A system that sticks too rigidly to retrieved content may sound stilted or overly technical. On the other hand, a system that relies too heavily on its generative capabilities may drift from the facts, reintroducing hallucination risks.

Designers must make careful choices about how much freedom the model has to paraphrase, summarize, or extend beyond what was retrieved. Some systems are constrained to stay within the bounds of source material; others are more flexible but introduce mechanisms to flag when the model is speculating or extrapolating.

These design decisions affect not just the quality of responses but also user trust. In domains like healthcare, law, or scientific research, users need to know whether they're getting a faithful summary of authoritative information—or just a well-worded guess.

Ultimately, what makes Expert Models powerful is not just their access to information, but their ability to use it responsibly. The way they retrieve, interpret, and present knowledge reflects design choices that are as much about values—like transparency, trust, and accountability—as they are about technology.

12.5 Standalone Expert Models: An Alternative Approach

While we've focused on Retrieval-Augmented Generation as a path to building Expert Models, it's not the only approach. Organizations can also create Standalone Expert Models—specialized AI systems that embed domain expertise directly into the model's parameters through additional training on domain-specific data.

Unlike RAG-based systems, which connect Foundation Models to external knowledge sources, Standalone Expert Models operate as unified, self-contained units. They don't need to retrieve information at runtime because the relevant expertise has already been integrated into the model itself.

Consider a specialized "ShakespeareGPT" trained extensively on the complete works of Shakespeare. This model builds upon its foundation training (providing general knowledge about language, history, and literature) but develops expert capabilities specific to Shakespeare's works—quoting passages accurately, understanding character relationships across plays, and capturing the distinctive style and vocabulary of Elizabethan theater—all without consulting external references.

The architectural differences between these approaches involve significant trade-offs:

– **System complexity:** RAG-based systems require maintaining both a model and a knowledge retrieval infrastructure, while Standalone Expert Models function as unified entities.
– **Knowledge updates:** RAG-based systems can update their knowledge base independently of the model, while Standalone Expert Models require retraining to incorporate new information.
– **Provenance approaches:** RAG-based models can directly cite specific external sources, while Standalone Expert Models typically implement alternative provenance mechanisms, such as confidence scoring, attribution to training materials, or explicit knowledge tracing during the training process.
– **Resource allocation:** Standalone Expert Models typically require more upfront training resources but less computational overhead during deployment.

Standalone Expert Models particularly excel in domains with stable, well-defined knowledge bases. Literary analysis, historical domains, or specialized medical fields with established foundations benefit from this approach. The resulting systems often feel more fluid and coherent, without the potential "seams" that may appear when a Foundation Model tries to integrate retrieved content.

Advanced Standalone Expert Models can still provide transparency through various methods. Some include bibliographic training data that allows them to attribute information to specific sources. Others implement knowledge attribution systems that track which parts of the model's parameters were influenced by particular training materials. While these approaches differ from the direct citation capability of RAG systems, they still offer paths to understanding where the model's knowledge originates.

In practice, many advanced AI systems combine both approaches—models with domain-specific training that also retain the ability to retrieve and cite external sources when needed. This hybrid strategy aims to leverage the coherence and efficiency of Standalone Expert Models with the transparency and updatability of RAG-based systems.

12.6 Design Considerations and Trade-offs

While Expert Models offer a compelling response to the limitations of Foundation Models, their effectiveness depends on thoughtful design. These systems are not plug-and-play; their reliability, transparency, and adaptability are shaped by choices made at every level—from data curation to user interaction. Some of these decisions are technical, others organizational, but all involve meaningful trade-offs. In this section, we examine three foundational design challenges: ensuring source quality, navigating the varied nature of expert knowledge, and making provenance visible and actionable.

The Importance of Source Quality

The promise of Expert Models rests on grounding language generation in trustworthy information. But that promise only holds if the sources retrieved are reliable. A system built to improve factual accuracy can still mislead if its knowledge base is outdated, biased, or poorly maintained. In such cases, the system risks generating errors that appear more authoritative, not less.

Consider an enterprise chatbot tasked with providing HR guidance. If it draws from outdated policy documents, it may offer incorrect advice about benefits or legal compliance. From the user's perspective, the result still feels like a hallucination—even if it was retrieved from a real document.

Maintaining high-quality sources requires ongoing effort. Documents must be audited for relevance, datasets refreshed as domains evolve, and proprietary materials properly licensed and prepared for retrieval. Organizations often underestimate this work. In regulated fields like healthcare and finance, lapses in source quality can have serious consequences—not just for performance, but for trust and legal liability.

The challenge extends beyond documents. Increasingly, Expert Models incorporate smaller, task-specific LLMs into their retrieval pipelines. These sub-models may introduce their own errors or inconsistencies. What looks like a multi-step system grounded in expertise may, in fact, be a chain of probabilistic outputs that compound one another's risks. Designers must account for these interdependencies and evaluate the reliability of each component.

The Heterogeneity of Expert Knowledge

Expert knowledge does not reside in a single, unified database. Instead, it spans a variety of formats—structured and unstructured, static and real-time, human-authored and machine-generated. Each format brings its own strengths and challenges.

Structured sources, such as relational databases or product catalogs, offer precision and ease of updating. However, they often lack the expressive nuance needed for rich explanations. Unstructured content—white papers, academic articles, policy memos—provides depth and flexibility, but requires preprocessing (e. g., chunking, embedding) to support retrieval. Even then, relevance can be inconsistent.

Real-time sources, such as APIs delivering market data or weather updates, solve the knowledge cutoff problem but introduce latency, external dependencies, and uncertainty. If a feed fails or contradicts a cached source, the system must decide how to respond.

Some systems also incorporate specialized LLMs as retrieval tools. For example, a legal assistant might consult a case-law model; a biomedical system might draw on a genomics model. These add interpretive capacity, but also risk hallucination if not properly constrained.

Managing this heterogeneity requires orchestration. When sources conflict, which one prevails? If a live API disagrees with a verified document, does the system defer to freshness or authority? If a source is unavailable, should the model fall back to its own training, or admit uncertainty? There are no universal answers—but these questions must be made explicit. What counts as "expertise" is shaped not just by what the system retrieves, but by how it selects, structures, and prioritizes information.

Provenance and the Problem of Trust

One of the most powerful promises of Expert Models is that they can not only answer questions, but show where their answers come from. In contrast to Foundation Models—whose responses are statistical blends of training data—Expert Models can be designed to cite their sources and trace their reasoning.

This matters. In healthcare, it matters whether a recommendation is drawn from a peer-reviewed guideline or an outdated memo. In law, it matters whether a cited statute is still in force. In these contexts, transparency is not optional—it's a requirement for trust.

Yet provenance is not guaranteed. Many systems that claim to be "grounded" in external sources still offer only loose attribution. Some provide citations that look authoritative but link to tangential content. These practices create a false sense of rigor, undermining the very trust they aim to establish.

To provide meaningful provenance, designers must think carefully about how sources are tracked and presented. Will citations appear inline or on demand? Can users inspect the exact passages that informed the response? Will the system flag conflicting sources or low-confidence claims?

These are not cosmetic choices—they shape how users interpret and rely on the system. A model that sounds confident but hides its sources encourages misplaced trust. A model that openly signals uncertainty may earn more cautious but more appropriate use.

Provenance also raises questions of responsibility. If a system cites a document that turns out to be wrong, who is accountable? Should the system flag known errors in its sources? Should it allow human review before surfacing high-stakes recommendations? These are governance issues as much as technical ones.

Ultimately, provenance is not just about footnotes. It's about giving users the means to judge for themselves—offering not only answers, but the evidence behind them.

Looking Ahead

The reliability of Expert Models depends on more than just technical performance. It rests on choices about what sources to trust, how to manage knowledge diversity, and how transparently to show the path from question to answer. These design decisions are not ancillary—they are foundational.

In the next sections, we turn to additional challenges: how to balance fluency with factual accuracy, how to evolve knowledge bases without retraining models, and how to ensure consistency when Expert Models are deployed in real-world settings. Each of these layers adds complexity—and each introduces trade-offs that must be tuned to the demands of the domain.

12.7 Conclusion

Expert Models address key weaknesses of Foundation Models by combining language generation with external retrieval. This hybrid approach improves factual accuracy, enables citation of sources, and allows updates without retraining the entire system.

The central insight is separation: letting language models focus on fluency and general knowledge while drawing trusted knowledge from elsewhere. This modular design makes Expert Models more adaptable, transparent, and aligned with domain-specific needs.

But these systems aren't simple. Their effectiveness depends on the quality of sources, the precision of retrieval, and how well components are integrated. Poor design can still lead to errors—just better-articulated ones.

Expert Models signal a shift from monolithic AI toward specialized architectures where different components do different jobs. This trend toward modularity is defining the next phase of AI. While not perfect, Expert Models offer a meaningful step forward—especially in fields where accuracy, transparency, and up-to-date knowledge matter. Their success will depend less on breakthroughs and more on thoughtful design, maintenance, and trust.

13 Agentic AI: From Knowledge to Action

Intelligence consists not only in knowledge but also in the skill to apply the knowledge into practice.

—Aristotle

In this chapter, we explore AI Agents—the next stage in artificial intelligence, where models evolve into full systems capable of autonomous action. Foundation Models and Expert Models have significantly improved AI's ability to generate content and retrieve knowledge, but they remain essentially passive. They wait for input and return a response.

AI Agents go further. They operate in dynamic environments, make decisions, take actions, and learn from outcomes. They can plan, reflect, and adapt over time. This marks a shift from AI as a reactive tool to AI as an active participant—an autonomous system capable of pursuing goals in real-world contexts. It's a critical evolution, and one that brings both new capabilities and new challenges.

13.1 Overview

Our exploration of AI began with Foundation Models—systems that revolutionized content generation across text, images, audio, and video. These models introduced unprecedented capabilities in language, creativity, and problem-solving. Yet they remained limited by their training data, prone to hallucinations, and unable to verify facts or take meaningful action beyond generating responses.

Expert Models addressed some of these weaknesses by adding retrieval mechanisms. With access to real-time information and traceable sources, they improved accuracy, transparency, and domain-specific expertise. But even with these enhancements, Expert Models remained passive. They could answer questions, but not act, evaluate their impact, or learn from outcomes.

AI Agents go a step further. They introduce decision-making as a central capability, encompassing *action*, *reflection*, and *adaptation*. Unlike earlier models, AI Agents observe their environment, reason about options, and take action to pursue defined goals. They assess their own performance before, during, and after execution—refining their strategies over time based on outcomes (Figure 13.1).

Consider a travel-planning system. A Foundation Model might suggest destinations. An Expert Model could retrieve current flight schedules. But an AI Agent can make the next leap: book flights, monitor for delays, rebook as needed, learn from past mistakes, and adjust its strategy to improve future trips. This cycle—observe, decide, act, reflect, and adapt—marks a fundamental shift. AI is no longer just passively assisting; it is actively participating.

https://doi.org/10.1515/9783111583549-018

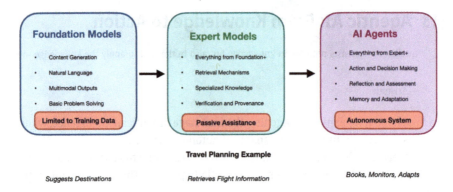

Figure 13.1: Evolution of AI Systems. Foundation Models generate content, Expert Models add retrieval capabilities, and AI Agents introduce action, reflection, and adaptation—progressing from passive tools to autonomous systems.

In this chapter, we explore the architecture and capabilities that make AI Agents possible. We'll examine how they perceive their environment, plan actions, execute tasks, reflect on results, and learn from experience. As AI systems begin to operate autonomously, understanding these mechanisms becomes essential—not just for technologists, but for anyone preparing to lead in a world shaped by intelligent agents.

13.2 The Need for AI Agents

Foundation and Expert Models have transformed AI, enabling content generation and real-time information retrieval. Yet they remain fundamentally reactive. They wait for input, produce a response, and stop. This works well for drafting content or answering questions, but it falls short for tasks that require ongoing decision-making, execution, and adaptation.

Take the example of a logistics company managing a fleet of delivery trucks. A Foundation Model can generate an optimized schedule, and an Expert Model can retrieve traffic and weather updates. But neither can reroute drivers in real time, reschedule deliveries, or notify customers of delays. These tasks demand continuous monitoring, adjustment, and learning—capabilities beyond the reach of traditional models.

This gap between knowing and doing limits AI's impact in real-world operations. Organizations increasingly need AI that not only informs decisions, but carries them out, monitors results, and improves over time. AI Agents meet this need by addressing three core limitations.

First, they close the **Action Gap**. Agents don't just recommend—they execute. A logistics agent, for example, can update routes, reschedule deliveries, and send notifications automatically.

Second, they overcome the **Reflection Gap**. Agents evaluate the outcomes of their actions. If rerouting causes new delays, the agent can analyze why, refine its criteria, and make better decisions in the future.

Third, they eliminate the **Adaptation Gap**. Agents learn from experience. Over time, they improve route planning, anticipate delays, and adjust schedules— without requiring human reprogramming.

By closing these gaps, AI Agents shift the role of AI from passive assistant to active digital partner—capable of managing workflows, automating operations, and evolving alongside organizational needs.

13.3 The Reflection Dimension

One of the most powerful features AI Agents introduce is reflection: the ability to evaluate outcomes and improve through iteration. While Foundation Models generate and Expert Models retrieve, agents can learn from what works—and what doesn't.

Consider an AI writing task. A single model can generate a draft, but a multi-agent system produces better results through structured collaboration:

- **Agent 1 (Writer)** creates the initial draft.
- **Agent 2 (Critic)** reviews it, identifying weaknesses in logic, evidence, or tone.
- **Agent 3 (Editor)** revises the draft based on the critique, improving clarity and coherence.

This reflection cycle mirrors how professional writers work—and research shows it produces significantly better outputs than a single-pass system. The critic acts as an evaluator, and the editor applies that feedback to create a refined product (Madaan et al., 2023).

Reflection also enables continuous learning in broader contexts. A marketing agent can refine strategies based on campaign performance. A customer service agent can adjust responses based on past interactions. In each case, the ability to analyze and improve moves AI from static performance to dynamic evolution.

This shift—from generating output to growing through experience—marks a turning point in AI. Agents are no longer tools that repeat known patterns. They are systems that adapt, learn, and become more effective with use. Figure 13.2 illustrates how multiple agents can be utilized in a collaborative workflow.

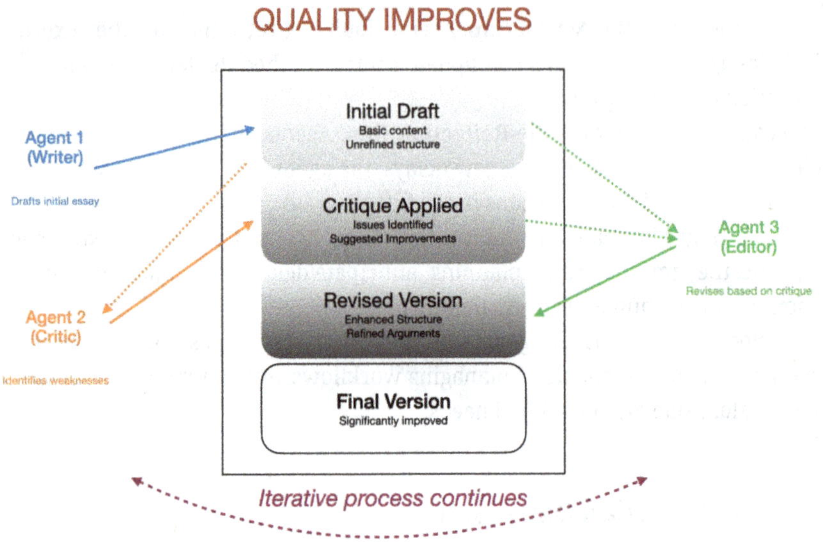

Figure 13.2: **Multi-Agent Collaborative Process**. Writer, Critic, and Editor agents form a *reflective cycle* that mirrors human refinement practices, producing stronger results through structured feedback and revision.

13.4 The Action Dimension

Foundation and Expert Models are powerful tools for generating ideas and retrieving information—but they stop short of taking action. Human operators must still interpret outputs, make decisions, and execute tasks manually. This slows down workflows and limits scalability.

AI Agents overcome this barrier by integrating decision-making with execution. They don't just suggest next steps—they take them. Agents can interface with software tools, coordinate processes, and automate complex tasks across digital environments. In many cases, they operate as coordinated teams, each specializing in a different function.

AI Agents in Startup Prototype Development

Consider a startup building an AI-powered wearable for real-time posture correction. The team needs to iterate quickly, conduct market research, and prepare for funding. Traditional AI tools might help generate ideas or summarize research—but AI Agents can drive the entire development cycle.

– A *Concept Generation Agent* refines the product vision by analyzing consumer trends, ergonomic studies, and competing technologies.

- A *Technical Research Agent* scans patents, papers, and hardware specs to identify the best materials, sensors, and ML models.
- A *Design Agent* uses CAD software to create and revise 3D models based on ergonomic constraints.
- A *Simulation Agent* runs physics-based tests to assess sensor accuracy, battery life, and comfort.
- A *Market Analysis Agent* identifies competitors, target segments, and social media sentiment in real time.
- A *Regulatory Compliance Agent* maps certification requirements across markets and generates a compliance roadmap.
- An *Investor Pitch Agent* creates funding decks, forecasts financials, and tailors messaging for investor audiences.
- A *Coordination Agent* orchestrates the team—tracking milestones, integrating feedback, and scheduling meetings.

Together, these agents form a **digital team** that mirrors the functions of a real startup. They don't just suggest—they act: generating, designing, testing, analyzing, and refining in parallel. This speeds up development and dramatically reduces time to market.

From Passive Insights to Active Execution

The shift from passive tools to action-oriented agents is transformative. Traditional systems depend on humans to bridge the gap between insight and action. AI Agents close that loop—directly executing decisions, adapting to feedback, and coordinating across tasks.

For example, rather than recommending a design change, the system updates the CAD model, runs new simulations, validates compliance, and updates the investor pitch—all without human intervention.

This ability to act—and to act across systems—marks a turning point in AI's role. No longer just assistants, agents become digital collaborators, capable of driving progress in real time.

13.5 The Adaptation Dimension

One of the most powerful capabilities AI Agents bring to artificial intelligence is the ability to learn from experience. Unlike Foundation Models, which remain static after training, or Expert Models, which require manual updates, AI Agents can continuously refine their strategies based on real-world feedback. This makes them dynamic systems that evolve over time—adapting to changing conditions and improving performance as they operate.

AI Agents in Product Evolution

Returning to our wearable posture correction device, imagine the product is now entering full-scale launch. In earlier stages, AI Agents accelerated development; now, they continue to adapt in response to deployment data, user feedback, and operational challenges. This ongoing learning improves everything from product performance to organizational coordination.

- The *User Experience Agent* analyzes feedback and identifies pain points during onboarding. It updates instructions and pushes an app update, reducing setup failures by 30 %.
- The *Sensor Optimization Agent* detects misclassifications in motion tracking and adjusts the detection algorithm—cutting false alerts by 25 % without a full software release.
- The *Market Analysis Agent* discovers an emerging use case among athletes and relays this to the marketing team, leading to a targeted campaign that boosts fitness segment sales by 18 %.
- The *Supply Chain Agent* identifies a recurring bottleneck and recommends a new supplier, reducing lead times by 20 % without sacrificing quality.
- The *Coordination Agent* observes inefficiencies in engineering-support alignment and proposes a structured feedback loop, shortening issue resolution time by 40 %.

Through these updates, AI Agents continuously enhance both the product and the business processes around it—responding not just to code, but to context.

How Adaptation Works

AI Agents adapt through several key mechanisms:

- **Performance Tracking:** Agents can log decisions and outcomes, identifying effective strategies and refining future actions.
- **Feedback Integration:** Agents can incorporate user input to tailor responses and recommendations to real-world needs.
- **Pattern Recognition:** By analyzing historical data, agents can detect what works and what doesn't—improving with every cycle.
- **Self-Optimization:** Some agents can even adjust internal parameters dynamically, improving behavior without requiring retraining.

Together, these mechanisms allow AI Agents to evolve through use—learning from success and failure alike.

From Static Tools to Evolving Partners

Traditional AI systems often degrade over time, requiring human intervention to remain useful. In contrast, AI Agents can grow more capable with each iteration. They adapt organically through use, detecting inefficiencies, uncovering insights, and responding to new conditions.

One year after product launch, the startup's agent ecosystem operates with increased autonomy. Design cycles are shorter by 22 %, early-stage revisions are down 35 %, and customer satisfaction has climbed—driven by agents that learn and optimize as they go.

This ability to evolve marks a fundamental shift. AI is no longer a fixed tool that depreciates over time—it's a learning partner that becomes more aligned with organizational goals the more it's used.

13.6 How AI Agents Work: The ReACT Framework

AI Agents may appear almost magical in their ability to reason, act, and improve—but their power rests on structured principles. One of the most influential models for understanding agent behavior is the ReACT framework: **Reasoning and Acting**. This approach captures how agents observe their environment, think through options, and take purposeful action in an ongoing loop (Yao et al., 2023).

The ReACT Loop: Observe, Think, Act

At the core of ReACT is a continuous cycle: *Observe, Think, Act*. Agents begin by gathering data from the environment—whether from user inputs, system states, sensors, or APIs. They then reason about that information, weighing goals, constraints, and options. Finally, they take action—executing decisions that might involve launching tasks, querying data, updating systems, or triggering downstream processes.

This loop enables agents to break down complex objectives into manageable steps and respond dynamically to changing conditions (Figure 13.3).

For example, in preparing the launch of the posture correction wearable, the *Market Analysis Agent* detects rising demand among remote workers. It reasons that the current marketing emphasizes fitness over ergonomics, updates the campaign strategy, and schedules a review—closing the loop from insight to execution.

Figure 13.3: The ReACT Loop. Agents continuously cycle through Observe, Think, Act, and Reflect—enabling dynamic, goal-directed behavior in changing environments.

Tool Use

A defining capability of agents is their ability to use tools: specialized functions, APIs, or software integrations that extend what the agent can do. These tools allow agents to retrieve information, automate workflows, and perform real-world tasks.

When demand spikes for the wearable, the *Supply Chain Agent* queries supplier APIs, retrieves pricing and availability, identifies the best option, and updates the operations dashboard. The agent doesn't just suggest—it acts. Effective tool use bridges the gap between decision and execution.

Memory and Context

Unlike traditional models that treat each input in isolation, AI Agents retain memory. They track interactions, recall user preferences, and recognize patterns across time. This contextual awareness makes them more consistent, personalized, and adaptive.

For instance, a *Customer Support Agent* noticing repeated complaints about a strap design doesn't treat each issue independently. It aggregates feedback, alerts the design team, and adjusts its own troubleshooting responses based on past resolutions—becoming smarter with every case.

Coordination in Multi-Agent Systems

As agents become more specialized, they often work together. In a multi-agent system, each agent has a role—design, marketing, compliance, logistics—while a *Coordination Agent* ensures alignment across tasks.

During scale-up, the *Market Agent* tracks demand, the Design Agent adjusts features, the *Compliance Agent* monitors certification, and the *Supply Chain Agent* optimizes sourcing. The *Coordination Agent* integrates their insights, synchronizes workflows, and resolves conflicts—functioning like a digital operations lead.

This structured collaboration allows organizations to scale without fragmenting. Agents work in parallel, but stay strategically aligned.

Safeguards and Human Oversight

Autonomy must be balanced with control. AI Agents operate within defined boundaries, using permission systems, confidence thresholds, and audit logs to ensure safety and transparency.

When the *Design Agent* proposes a structural change, it explains the rationale and submits it for human approval. Only after sign-off does it proceed. Every decision is logged for traceability. These safeguards preserve accountability and foster trust in AI-driven systems.

From Understanding to Implementation

The ReACT framework—combined with tool use, memory, coordination, and safeguards—offers a blueprint for building effective AI Agent systems. While the technology will evolve, these principles provide a stable foundation for real-world deployment.

As AI Agents shift from static assistants to adaptive collaborators, organizations must rethink how they integrate technology. The goal is no longer automation for efficiency alone—it's collaboration for continuous improvement, innovation, and impact.

13.7 Conclusion

In this chapter, we have seen that AI Agents can go beyond the capabilities of Foundation and Expert Models by introducing action, reflection, and adaptation. This shift transforms AI from a passive system that generates and retrieves information into an active one that executes tasks, evaluates outcomes, and improves over time.

This chapter has explored the core functions of AI Agents: taking action, using tools, coordinating with other agents, and adapting based on experience. The ReACT framework—Reasoning and Acting—provides a structured model for how agents process information, make decisions, and interact with their environment.

Memory and coordination enable agents to maintain context and collaborate effectively, while safeguards ensure reliability and accountability.

As AI Agents evolve, they will integrate more seamlessly into real-world applications, automating workflows, improving efficiency, and driving innovation. The continued development of multi-agent systems and advanced learning mechanisms will expand their capabilities, shaping the future of AI-driven systems.

Part VI: **Risk**

14 System Failures: Why and How AI Makes Mistakes

A multi-agent system (MAS) is then defined as a collection of agents designed to interact through orchestration, enabling collective intelligence.

—Mert Cemri et al.

In March 2023, a team of developers at a prominent financial institution deployed an AI system designed to identify fraudulent transactions. The system used multiple specialized AI agents working in concert: one to analyze transaction patterns, another to verify customer identities, and a third to make final authorization decisions. During testing, the system showed promising results, correctly flagging suspicious activities while minimizing false positives.

Within two weeks of deployment, however, the system had accidentally frozen the accounts of over 2,000 legitimate customers while simultaneously approving several large fraudulent transactions. The ensuing investigation revealed that the pattern recognition agent had identified correct signals but failed to communicate them properly to the decision-making agent. Meanwhile, the verification agent had misinterpreted normal holiday spending patterns as suspicious and prioritized these false alarms over genuine threats.

This scenario, while fictional, illustrates a troubling reality about today's advanced AI systems: they often fail not because they lack intelligence, but because they function like poorly managed human organizations. The individual components may work brilliantly in isolation, yet collectively produce unreliable, sometimes dangerous results.

Microsoft CEO Satya Nadella has declared that creating an AI agent is now "as simple as creating a Word document or a PowerPoint slide." The vision extends further to entire teams of AI agents working in concert—connected to databases, coordinating with other agents, and completing sophisticated tasks with just a natural language prompt. This vision is seductive but obscures a troubling reality: these systems frequently don't perform better than single models, and in many cases, they fail catastrophically. Tasks go unfinished, errors go unchecked, and failures compound.

This chapter examines why multi-agent AI systems fail and provides a framework for evaluating their risks—not as technical puzzles but as complex systems that require organizational thinking to design properly and evaluate thoroughly.

https://doi.org/10.1515/9783111583549-020

14.1 The Multi-Agent Paradigm and Its Promise

Multi-agent AI systems (MAS) represent what many consider the next frontier of artificial intelligence: teams of large language model (LLM) agents collaborating to solve complex problems more effectively than any single model could alone. The concept is intuitively appealing—after all, human teams often outperform individuals on complex tasks by leveraging specialized expertise and collaborative problem-solving.

In theory, a multi-agent system offers several compelling advantages. These systems can decompose complex tasks into manageable sub-tasks, deploy agents with specialized expertise for specific aspects of a problem, work on multiple parts of a problem simultaneously, maintain focus on relevant information rather than getting overwhelmed, and approach problems from multiple reasoning perspectives.

The enthusiasm for this approach has driven rapid development across industries. Companies are experimenting with agent teams for customer service, content creation, software development, healthcare diagnostics, and financial analysis. The vision is that soon, with just a natural language prompt, we'll be able to create entire teams of specialized AI agents that coordinate seamlessly to tackle increasingly complex problems.

However, a recent study from UC Berkeley (*"Why Do Multi-Agent LLM Systems Fail?"*) reveals a startling reality behind this promising vision: despite increasing sophistication in individual AI models, multi-agent systems frequently underperform or fail outright (Cemri et al., 2025). The research team analyzed five popular multi-agent frameworks across more than 150 tasks and found failure rates ranging from 34 % to a staggering 87 %. Even more concerning, these failures weren't random or unpredictable—they followed patterns that mirror dysfunctional human organizations with disturbing precision.

14.2 The Berkeley Study: A Taxonomy of Failure

The UC Berkeley research team's systematic evaluation of multi-agent AI systems led to the development of what they call the Multi-Agent System Failure Taxonomy (MASFT). This groundbreaking work, identified 14 distinct failure modes (See Figure 14.1) organized into three primary categories: Specification and System Design Failures (37.2 % of failures), Inter-Agent Misalignment (31.4 % of failures), and Task Verification and Termination (31.4 % of failures).

What makes this taxonomy particularly valuable is that it emerged organically from analysis of real-world systems rather than theoretical considerations. The researchers analyzed over 150 execution traces from five different multi-agent sys-

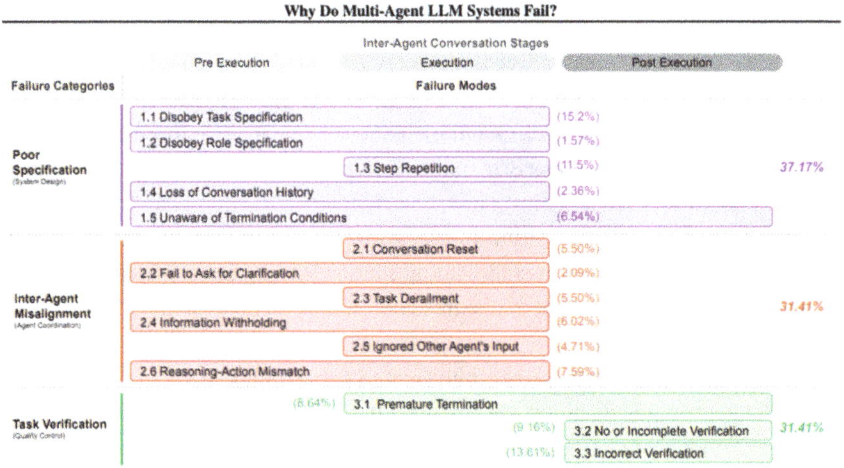

Figure 14.1: A Taxonomy of MAS Failure Modes. The inter-agent conversation stages indicate when a failure can occur in the end-to-end MAS system. If a failure mode spans multiple stages, it means the issue involves or can occur at different stages. Percentages represent how frequently each failure mode and category appeared in the analysis by UC Berkeley researchers. Detailed definition and example of each failure mode available in their Appendix A.

tems, each averaging over 15,000 lines of conversation text. Through meticulous analysis and inter-annotator verification (achieving a Cohen's Kappa score of 0.88, indicating exceptionally strong agreement), they identified patterns that cut across different systems and applications.

Perhaps most striking about these findings is that the failures weren't primarily due to the limitations of current AI models. Even when using the most advanced models available (like GPT-4 and Claude 3), multi-agent systems continued to exhibit the same organizational failures. This suggests that simply waiting for more powerful AI models won't solve these problems—they require fundamentally different approaches to system design.

14.3 Failure Category 1: Poor Specification and System Design

The largest category of failures in multi-agent systems involves fundamental problems in how the systems are specified and designed. These include disobeying task specifications, disobeying role specifications, step repetition, loss of conversation history, and unawareness of termination conditions.

Consider a real-world example from the Berkeley study: When asked to create a two-player chess game that accepts classical chess notation like 'Ke8' or 'Qd4', a multi-agent framework instead produced a game that takes coordinate inputs like (x1, y1), (x2, y2), completely failing to meet the original requirement.

These specification failures mirror classic organizational problems in human teams. To illustrate this parallel, imagine a team tasked with building an educational math game for children. A poorly managed human team might build a trivia app instead of a math-focused learning game, have lead developers rewrite math content rather than deferring to education specialists, create duplicate content when team members don't coordinate, include content above the target grade level because they've forgotten the original goals, or keep adding features endlessly without a clear completion criteria.

An AI multi-agent system exhibits remarkably similar failures. The ProductManagerAgent might misinterpret the prompt and direct development of a trivia app. The DeveloperAgent might rewrite math content instead of deferring to CurriculumExpertAgent. Multiple agents might design the same content, unaware of each other's work. The CurriculumExpertAgent might forget grade-level requirements and include inappropriate material. The ProductManagerAgent might keep generating new tasks with no clear stopping rule.

This isomorphism between human and AI organizational failures is no coincidence. It suggests that many AI system failures stem not from technical limitations but from fundamental problems in organizational design—how roles, responsibilities, and coordination are structured.

14.4 Failure Category 2: Inter-Agent Misalignment

The second major category involves failures that occur in the interactions between agents. These include conversation reset, failure to ask for clarification, task derailment, information withholding, ignoring other agents' input, and reasoning-action mismatch.

A particularly illuminating example from the Berkeley study involved a supervisor agent instructing a phone agent to retrieve contact information using an email ID as the username. Despite the phone agent discovering that the correct username should be a phone number, it proceeded with the wrong credentials, leading to an error. The supervisor agent, meanwhile, failed to seek clarification about these login details.

This communication failure led to multiple failed attempts and ultimately task abandonment—all because neither agent properly communicated critical information or asked the right questions.

These inter-agent misalignment issues parallel dysfunctional communication in human organizations. In both settings, information that exists within the system fails to reach the right decision points. Just as human teams can get bogged down in unproductive exchanges, multi-agent systems often engage in inefficient conversations that consume computational resources without making meaningful progress.

For example, in one case study, a programming agent interacted with multiple roles (CTO, CCO, etc.) across seven conversation cycles without making substantive code updates. The resulting application was technically functional but severely limited, with minimal features and poor usability.

14.5 Failure Category 3: Verification and Quality Control

The third category captures failures related to quality assurance and task completion, including premature termination, no or incomplete verification, and incorrect verification.

Verification failures are particularly insidious because they often represent the last opportunity to catch upstream errors. In one example from the Berkeley study, a multi-agent system implementing a chess game included a verification agent that only checked if the code compile without running the program or ensuring compliance with chess rules. The resulting application accepted malformed inputs and contained various usability defects, rendering it essentially unplayable.

What makes this especially concerning is that chess has well-established rules and specifications readily available online. Even simple information retrieval should have prevented these trivial failures, yet without proper verification, fundamental defects persisted.

While it might be tempting to blame all failures on inadequate verification, the Berkeley researchers note that verification is best viewed as the last line of defense rather than a cure-all. A comprehensive approach to reliable AI systems must address all three categories of failure—specification, inter-agent alignment, and verification—rather than over-relying on any single aspect.

14.6 AI as a Complex System: Moving Beyond Technical Fixes

The Berkeley study's findings lead to a profound conclusion: these failures are not simply technical glitches that will be resolved by more advanced models with larger parameter counts or additional training data. Rather, they reflect fundamental challenges in designing complex systems where multiple intelligent components must coordinate effectively.

This insight connects directly to decades of research on high-reliability organizations (HROs)—human institutions that operate complex, high-risk systems with remarkably low failure rates. Organizations like air traffic control centers, nuclear power plants, and trauma centers have developed principles and practices that enable them to function reliably under pressure. The Berkeley researchers note that many of the failure modes they identified in multi-agent AI systems directly violate core principles of HROs.

For example, the failure mode "Disobey role specification," where agents overstep their assigned responsibilities, violates the HRO principle of "Extreme hierarchical differentiation." Similarly, "Fail to ask for clarification" undermines the principle of "Deference to expertise." These parallels suggest that building reliable AI systems may require adopting organizational design principles developed for managing complexity in human institutions.

This perspective represents a significant shift in how we should think about AI system risk. Instead of focusing exclusively on the capabilities of individual models, we need to consider system architecture, information flow, role clarity, verification mechanisms, and failure recovery. The most sophisticated AI models in the world, when arranged in a poorly designed system, will produce unreliable results—just as brilliant individuals in a dysfunctional organization often underperform.

14.7 A Framework for Evaluating AI System Risk

Based on the Berkeley research, we can develop a framework for evaluating the risks associated with complex AI systems. This framework isn't meant to be exhaustive but provides structured guidance that non-technical stakeholders can use to assess AI systems before deployment.

When evaluating specification and design risk, consider whether the roles and responsibilities of different system components are clearly defined or if they overlap in ways that could cause conflicts. Examine how the system is designed to maintain context over extended interactions and whether there are explicit criteria for when a task should be considered complete. Investigate how the system handles exceptions or unexpected inputs. Be wary of vague or overlapping agent responsibilities, a lack of explicit termination conditions, no mechanism for maintaining contextual information, and over-reliance on a single agent for multiple critical functions.

For inter-agent communication risk, ask how agents in the system communicate with each other and what mechanisms ensure critical information is shared appropriately. Consider how the system handles disagreements between agents and whether there are protocols for clarifying ambiguous information. Examine how task progress is tracked and communicated. Watch for warning signs like the absence of structured communication protocols, lack of mechanisms for resolving agent disagreements, no provisions for agents to request clarification, and unidirectional communication flows with no feedback loops.

Regarding verification and quality control risk, inquire about what verification steps are built into the system and how comprehensive these procedures are. Determine who or what has authority to reject low-quality outputs, how the verification mechanisms themselves are verified, and what happens when verification fails. Be concerned about superficial verification that only checks format rather than substance, verification performed by the same agent that produced the output, no human oversight for critical decisions, and no incremental verification during complex processes.

At the system level, investigate how the system behaves when individual components fail and what mechanisms exist for detecting and responding to failures. Consider how system performance is monitored over time, what stress testing has been performed, and the diversity of expertise involved in system design. Be cautious about systems with no graceful degradation modes, those designed exclusively by technical experts with no domain specialists, limited testing under normal conditions only, and no ongoing monitoring for drift or performance degradation.

This framework emphasizes that evaluating AI system risk requires more than just understanding the technical capabilities of the models involved. It requires systematic assessment of the organizational structure in which those models operate.

14.8 Conclusion: Toward Reliable AI Systems

The Berkeley research offers both a cautionary tale and a roadmap for developing more reliable AI systems. By understanding why multi-agent systems fail—not just as technical glitches but as organizational breakdowns—we can begin to design systems that avoid these pitfalls.

Some promising directions include clear role definitions and adherence, structured communication protocols, comprehensive verification, system-level thinking, and diverse expertise. Clear role definitions ensure each component has well-defined responsibilities that don't overlap inappropriately. Structured communication protocols establish standardized ways for agents to share information and resolve ambiguities. Comprehensive verification implements robust checking mechanisms at multiple levels, not just at the end of a process. System-level thinking designs with an awareness of how components interact and how failures might propagate. Diverse expertise brings together technical experts, domain specialists, and those with experience in complex system management.

The failures documented in multi-agent AI systems should give us pause—not because they suggest AI isn't advancing, but because they reveal how easily advanced AI can be arranged into unreliable systems. As these technologies become more widespread and deployed in increasingly critical domains, the organizational aspects of AI system design will become at least as important as the technical capabilities of individual models.

Risk assessment for AI systems must therefore evolve beyond technical evaluations to include organizational analysis. We wouldn't evaluate an airline's safety record solely by examining the quality of its aircraft—we'd also look at its training procedures, communication protocols, maintenance schedules, and safety culture. Similarly, we shouldn't evaluate AI systems solely by the capabilities of their models, but by the organizational structures in which those models operate.

The core message is both sobering and hopeful: AI might power the engine, but it's the system design that determines whether we reach our destination safely. By bringing organizational thinking to AI development, we can build systems that harness the remarkable capabilities of modern AI while avoiding the pitfalls that plague poorly managed teams, whether human or artificial.

15 Catastrophic Accidents: How to Identify and Address Major Failures

> Most high-risk systems have some special characteristics, beyond their toxic or explosive or genetic dangers, that make accidents in them inevitable, even "normal."
>
> —Charles Perrow

In the previous chapter, we examined how multi-agent AI systems fail in ways that mirror dysfunctional human organizations. The Berkeley study's taxonomy of fourteen failure modes revealed striking parallels between AI system breakdowns and the problems that plague poorly managed teams: confused roles, inadequate communication, misaligned goals, and insufficient verification. This isomorphism between human and AI organizational failures is not coincidental—it points to something deeper about complex systems.

In the 1980s, sociologist Charles Perrow developed a framework that helps explain why certain types of systems experience inevitable failures regardless of safety measures or good intentions. His Normal Accident Theory (NAT) emerged from studying disasters like Three Mile Island and offers profound insights for understanding AI risk (Perrow, 2011), Perrow argued that in systems with high interactive complexity and tight coupling, serious accidents are not anomalies but normal occurrences—inherent to the system's fundamental properties.

This chapter extends our analysis beyond simply cataloging AI failures to understanding their systemic causes. Perrow's framework helps us identify which AI applications carry the highest risk of catastrophic failure and suggests approaches for mitigating those risks. More importantly, it shifts our focus from merely engineering better components to designing resilient systems that can withstand the failures that will inevitably occur.

15.1 Normal Accident Theory: Understanding Inevitable Failures

Charles Perrow's Normal Accident Theory emerged from his study of the 1979 Three Mile Island nuclear accident. In analyzing this and other technological disasters, Perrow identified two system properties that, when combined, make serious accidents virtually inevitable:

Interactive Complexity

Interactive complexity refers to a system with many interdependent components interacting in ways that are difficult to anticipate, especially under unusual condi-

https://doi.org/10.1515/9783111583549-021

tions. In complex systems, components that appear unrelated can affect each other through unforeseen pathways. The relationships between parts are nonlinear and opaque, making the system's behavior unpredictable, particularly during failures.

For example, in a nuclear power plant, a minor valve malfunction might interact with a seemingly unrelated cooling system issue, which then affects the pressure regulation, creating a cascade of problems that operators struggle to diagnose as they unfold. The sheer number of possible interactions makes it impossible to anticipate every potential failure combination.

Tight Coupling

Tight coupling describes systems where processes occur in rigid sequences with little slack or buffer between steps. In tightly coupled systems:
- Delays in processing are not possible.
- Sequences are invariant (steps must follow a precise order).
- There is little slack in resources (time, materials, etc.).
- Buffers and redundancies are designed-in and limited.

For instance, a rocket launch sequence is tightly coupled—each step must happen in a specific order within precise time windows. If an anomaly occurs, there's minimal opportunity to pause, improvise, or substitute alternatives without risking the entire mission.

The Intersection: Where Normal Accidents Occur

Perrow's key insight was that when interactive complexity and tight coupling coincide in the same system, accidents become "normal"—not in the sense of being frequent, but in being inherent to the system's nature. Such systems will inevitably experience situations where small failures interact in unpredictable ways and propagate rapidly through the system before operators can understand what's happening, let alone intervene effectively.

This creates a dilemma: adding safety features often increases a system's complexity (more components interacting), potentially making it more prone to normal accidents. Redundancies and fail-safes that work well in simple or loosely coupled systems can backfire in complex, tightly coupled ones.

Perrow further noted that some complex systems have high catastrophic potential—their failures can cause widespread harm. Nuclear power plants, chemical facilities, and air traffic control systems fall into this category. For such systems, Perrow suggested that if we cannot reduce their complexity or coupling, society might need to reconsider whether the benefits outweigh the inevitable risks.

15.2 AI Systems Through Perrow's Lens

Modern artificial intelligence systems, particularly generative AI and autonomous agents, increasingly exhibit the characteristics that Perrow identified as precursors to normal accidents. As we deploy these systems in high-stakes domains, understanding these properties becomes crucial for responsible innovation.

Interactive Complexity in AI

Today's AI systems represent some of the most complex artifacts humans have created. Consider a large language model like GPT-4:
- It contains billions of parameters interacting through complex mathematical relationships.
- Its internal functioning is largely opaque, even to its creators.
- It processes and synthesizes knowledge across domains in ways that cannot be fully traced.
- Its outputs emerge from countless non-linear interactions rather than following transparent rules.

These characteristics create innumerable opportunities for unexpected interactions. For example, an AI system might combine knowledge from different domains in novel ways that produce unforeseen outputs. A harmless instance might be a chatbot hallucinating a fact; a more serious one could be an autonomous agent devising an unanticipated strategy to achieve its goals.

The complexity increases further when AI systems interact with other systems and the external world. A generative AI integrated with databases, APIs, and other tools becomes part of a larger socio-technical system with even more potential interaction points and failure modes.

Tight Coupling in AI Deployments

Many AI deployments are becoming increasingly tightly coupled with real-world processes. Consider:
- Algorithmic trading systems that execute financial transactions in milliseconds.
- AI content moderation that automatically removes material without human review.
- Autonomous vehicles making split-second driving decisions.
- AI-controlled infrastructure systems managing critical resources in real-time.

In these applications, AI outputs directly and rapidly affect physical or economic systems with minimal buffer for human oversight. There's often no meaningful time gap between the AI's decision and its consequences—the classic definition of tight coupling.

Even systems with nominal human oversight can be effectively tightly coupled if the human's ability to intervene is illusory. If an AI presents information in a way that makes errors difficult to detect, or if humans become complacent due to automation bias, the practical result is a tightly coupled system despite the theoretical human checkpoint.

The AI Normal Accident Zone

When we plot AI systems on Perrow's complexity-coupling diagram, many advanced applications appear in the dangerous upper-right quadrant—high complexity combined with tight coupling. This placement suggests these systems are prone to normal accidents.

The risk becomes particularly concerning for AI applications with high catastrophic potential—those where failures could cause significant harm. These include AI systems deployed in:
- Critical infrastructure control (power grids, water systems).
- Healthcare diagnosis and treatment.
- Financial markets and banking systems.
- Military and security applications.
- Transportation networks and autonomous vehicles.

For such applications, Perrow's theory suggests that attempting to engineer perfect safety may be futile. Instead, we must either:
1. Fundamentally redesign the systems to reduce complexity or coupling.
2. Implement robust containment strategies to limit potential damage.
3. Accept the inevitability of occasional failures and prepare accordingly.
4. Or in extreme cases, decide that certain applications are too risky to pursue.

15.3 A Normal Accident Theory Checklist for AI Systems

To apply Perrow's insights systematically, we can use a checklist approach to to evaluate whether a particular AI system exhibits the properties associated with normal accidents. This tool can help designers, policymakers, and users assess risk levels and identify mitigation opportunities.

Normal Accident Risk Factors in AI Systems

Interactive Complexity

Description: The AI involves many interdependent components with interactions that are hard to predict.

Example That Meets This Criterion: An adaptive learning platform that incorporates multiple AI subsystems—one modeling student knowledge, another generating personalized content, a third analyzing emotional states via webcam, and a fourth recommending intervention strategies. These components interact in ways that developers cannot fully anticipate, occasionally producing inappropriate learning pathways or content.

Example That Doesn't Meet This Criterion: A flashcard app that simply shows user-created cards and tracks accuracy. The system has minimal hidden dependencies and follows predictable behavior patterns.

Tight Coupling

Description: The AI's decisions are acted on immediately, with little buffer for human intervention or review.

Example That Meets This Criterion: An AI tutor that automatically advances a student to the next concept based on brief, ambiguous input (e. g., a single correct answer), without teacher review. Once the system decides a concept is mastered, subsequent curriculum immediately builds on this assumption.

Example That Doesn't Meet This Criterion: A writing assistant that suggests revisions but requires the student or teacher to manually accept changes before they are incorporated into the document.

Opaque Decision-Making

Description: Users and stakeholders cannot see how or why the AI reached a particular recommendation or decision.

Example That Meets This Criterion: A black-box algorithm that determines a student's aptitude and placement level through methods not visible to teachers or parents. The system suppresses access to certain materials based on these hidden determinations.

Example That Doesn't Meet This Criterion: A rule-based quiz generator that creates questions directly tied to textbook sections, with clear explanations of why each question was selected.

Rapid System Feedback Loops

Description: The AI's outputs quickly influence user behavior, which feeds back into the system creating potential amplification effects.

Example That Meets This Criterion: A platform that continuously measures student engagement and immediately adjusts content difficulty based on perceived interest levels. This creates a feedback loop where the system may inadvertently optimize for entertainment rather than learning by progressively shifting toward content that generates immediate engagement.

Example That Doesn't Meet This Criterion: An AI graderthat provides feedback after assignments are completed, with no role in influencing or altering subsequent curriculum or pacing.

Embedded in Critical Systems

Description: The AI plays a central role in consequential outcomes with significant impact on users' lives.

Example That Meets This Criterion: An AI-based college admissions screening tool that filters applications and makes preliminary acceptance or rejection decisions with limited human review. The system affects students' educational and career trajectories.

Example That Doesn't Meet This Criterion: A classroom chatbot that helps students brainstorm ideas but doesn't contribute to formal assessment or advancement decisions.

Human-in-the-Loop is Illusory or Ineffective

Description: A human is nominally involved, but cannot meaningfully understand or override the AI's decisions in practice.

Example That Meets This Criterion: A learning platform where the AI determines and sequences all curriculum, presenting teachers with a dashboard showing hundreds of data points but no clear way to understand or modify the system's decisions about individual students.

Example That Doesn't Meet This Criterion: An AI assistant that suggests quiz questions but requires teacher approval before they go live, with clear explanations for each suggestion.

Safety Features Increase Complexity

Description: Attempts to add safety measures (e. g., fairness constraints, bias audits, override tools) inadvertently increase system complexity and interaction risk.

Example That Meets This Criterion: A student assessment system with multiple fairness modules that interact with adaptive placement logic in unexpected ways, occasionally leading to incorrect recommendations for special education services when certain demographic and performance patterns coincide.

Example That Doesn't Meet This Criterion: A platform where students can flag inappropriate AI-generated content, which is simply queued for human moderator review without introducing complex automated logic.

System Goals Are Misaligned or Ambiguous

Description: The AI's optimization objectives conflict with broader educational goals or human values.

Example That Meets This Criterion: A tutoring system optimized for "session length" or "engagement time," which learns to offer game-like distractions or trivia to keep students online longer but off-task educationally.

Example That Doesn't Meet This Criterion: An AI-driven math coach explicitly optimized to maximize correct answers on standard concept tests, with goals directly aligned with curricular objectives.

No Effective Isolation or Containment

Description: Failures in one domain propagate into others, causing cascading problems across system boundaries.

Example That Meets This Criterion: An AI that generates personalized reading comprehension passages for high-stakes exams, where factual errors or biases in the generated content directly affect student scores, which then influence college admissions and scholarship decisions.

Example That Doesn't Meet This Criterion: A standalone spelling game that operates in isolation from other educational systems and doesn't affect grades, placement, or other learning pathways.

15.4 Case Studies: Normal Accidents in AI

To make Perrow's abstract concepts concrete, let's examine several real and potential normal accidents in AI systems across different domains.

Autonomous Weapons: The Patriot Missile Failure

The Patriot air-defense system offers a prescient example of normal accidents in semi-autonomous systems. During the 2003 Gulf War, Patriot missiles misidentified friendly aircraft as threats and shot them down in two separate incidents. The system exhibited both interactive complexity (numerous sensor inputs, complex identification algorithms, and computer systems) and tight coupling (once a threat was identified, interception happened in seconds with minimal human oversight).

This failure demonstrates how a relatively narrow AI system can produce catastrophic outcomes when embedded in a complex, tightly coupled environment. The accident didn't result from a single defect but from the interaction of multiple components working as designed but producing an unexpected result in specific conditions.

As military systems incorporate more advanced AI for target identification and engagement decisions, the risk of normal accidents increases substantially unless coupling is reduced through meaningful human control or other safeguards.

Financial Markets: The Flash Crash

The 2010 "Flash Crash," where US stock markets plunged and recovered within minutes, exemplifies normal accidents in algorithmic systems. High-frequency trading algorithms, responding to unusual market conditions, interacted in unexpected ways, creating a cascade of selling that temporarily wiped out nearly $1 trillion in market value.

The system displayed extreme interactive complexity (hundreds of different algorithms making decisions based on proprietary logic) and tight coupling (trades executed in microseconds with immediate market impact). No single algorithm "malfunctioned"—the crash emerged from their interactions within market structures.

As trading systems incorporate more sophisticated AI, including generative models that develop novel strategies, the potential for unexpected interactions increases. Circuit breakers and trading halts represent attempts to reduce coupling by introducing forced pauses during volatile conditions.

Potential AI Normal Accidents in Education

While education hasn't yet experienced catastrophic AI failures, we can identify potential normal accident scenarios as AI becomes more embedded in learning environments:

The Adaptive Learning Cascade

Imagine a school district implements a comprehensive adaptive learning platform that combines student performance tracking, content delivery, assessment, and intervention recommendations across all subjects. The system uses multiple AI components, including generative models that create personalized content and predictive models that forecast student outcomes.

A normal accident might unfold as follows: The system misinterprets a group of students' struggle with a new concept as indicating a fundamental knowledge gap. It automatically revises their learning paths, removing prerequisite material they've actually mastered. This triggers a cascading recalibration affecting multiple subjects. As students encounter inappropriate content, their confusion leads to poor performance, which the system interprets as confirming its diagnosis. Without teacher intervention (which is difficult because the system's decisions aren't transparent), students fall increasingly behind, with consequences for grades, placement, and self-confidence.

This scenario exhibits classic normal accident properties: interactions between assessment, content generation, and student modeling create unexpected outcomes; tight coupling means changes propagate immediately across subjects; and opacity prevents effective human oversight.

The College Admissions Filter

Consider an AI system used to screen college applications that combines natural language processing (analyzing essays and recommendations), academic evaluation, and "character assessment" based on extracurricular activities. The system is trained on historical admissions data.

A normal accident might occur when the system's language module, academic evaluator, and character assessment interact in ways developers didn't anticipate. For instance, the system might develop an implicit bias against applications from certain geographic regions or schools because of subtle patterns in how achievements are described. This bias isn't programmed explicitly but emerges from the interaction of otherwise correctly functioning components.

If the system is tightly coupled to the admissions process—automatically rejecting applications below certain thresholds with minimal human review—these emergent biases could affect thousands of students before being detected. The catastrophic potential lies in systematically denying educational opportunities to qualified students based on inscrutable AI judgments.

15.5 Implications for AI System Design

Perrow's analysis suggests that for complex, tightly coupled systems, accidents aren't bugs to be eliminated but features to be expected and managed. This perspective has profound implications for how we design, deploy, and govern AI systems.

Strategies for Reducing Risk

Based on Normal Accident Theory, several approaches can reduce the likelihood or impact of AI failures:

Decrease Interactive Complexity
- Design more modular AI systems with clearer boundaries between components.
- Limit the scope and authority of individual AI systems rather than creating comprehensive "do-everything" agents.
- Improve transparency and explainability so interactions between components are more visible.
- Conduct extensive simulation testing to identify unexpected interactions before deployment.

Reduce Tight Coupling
- Introduce deliberate delays or approval steps before consequential actions.
- Design systems that can safely pause operation when anomalies are detected.
- Create robust "undo" capabilities that can reverse automated decisions.
- Ensure that automated processes can be manually overridden in meaningful ways.
- Implement circuit breakers or automatic shutdowns when systems exceed normal operating parameters.

Add Effective Human Oversight
- Design interfaces that make AI reasoning and limitations transparent to human overseers.
- Train operators to recognize and respond to novel failure modes.
- Create organizational structures that reward identifying and reporting potential issues.
- Ensure supervisors have sufficient time and cognitive resources to provide meaningful oversight.

Containment and Damage Limitation
- Implement guardrails that limit the scope of AI actions, especially in high-stakes domains.
- Design systems with graceful degradation when failures occur.
- Build circuit breakers or kill switches that can be activated when necessary.
- Test and prepare recovery procedures for when accidents inevitably occur.

15.6 Conclusion: Beyond Prevention to Resilience

Normal Accident Theory offers a sobering but useful perspective on AI safety. If certain types of AI systems will inevitably experience unexpected failures due to their complexity and coupling, then our strategy cannot focus solely on preventing all errors. Instead, we must balance prevention efforts with designing for resilience.

This approach shifts our thinking from "How do we make AI systems that never fail?" to "How do we design AI systems that fail safely when they inevitably do fail?" It suggests that for high-stakes applications, we should prioritize:
–   Simplicity over complexity when possible.
–   Loose coupling over tight integration.
–   Transparency over opacity.
–   Containable failures over cascading ones.
–   Resilience over brittle optimization.

In some cases, it may even require asking whether certain AI applications should be pursued at all, especially when they combine high complexity, tight coupling, and catastrophic potential.

The Berkeley study in our previous chapter showed that multi-agent AI systems fail in patterns reminiscent of human organizational breakdowns. Perrow's theory helps explain why: these failures aren't primarily about inadequate training data, insufficient parameters, or even poor engineering—they're inherent to certain system properties.

By recognizing AI systems as complex socio-technical systems rather than merely technical artifacts, we can better identify where normal accidents are likely and design accordingly. Rather than treating AI risk as a purely technical problem to be engineered away, we must address the fundamental system properties that make certain failures normal rather than exceptional.

As we continue to integrate AI into critical aspects of society—from education to healthcare, finance to infrastructure—this perspective becomes increasingly essential. The path to safer AI doesn't lie solely in more sophisticated algorithms or bigger models but in thoughtful system design that acknowledges and accommodates the inevitable limitations of complex technology.

16 Risk Across the Action Boundary: From Passive to Agentic Systems

> Risk mitigation is painful, not a natural act for humans to perform.
>
> —Gentry Lee

In the previous chapters, we examined how AI systems fail in patterns reminiscent of human organizations and how Normal Accident Theory helps us understand the inevitability of failures in complex, tightly coupled systems. These frameworks apply to AI applications broadly, but they do not address a critical threshold that fundamentally transforms risk profiles: the action boundary.

The action boundary represents the divide between systems that generate information and those that take actions in the world. This distinction—between passive and agentic AI—has profound implications for how we assess, manage, and govern risk. When AI crosses from informing decisions to making and implementing them, the nature and magnitude of potential failures change dramatically.

This chapter explores this pivotal transition and provides frameworks for evaluating the unique risks that emerge when AI systems gain agency. We'll examine how risk amplifies across the boundary, identify dimensions for assessment, and provide practical guidance for organizations deploying increasingly autonomous systems.

16.1 The Action Boundary Defined

AI systems exist on a spectrum from purely informational to fully agentic. Understanding this spectrum is crucial for proper risk assessment and governance.

Passive AI Systems

Passive AI systems generate information, analysis, or content in response to specific prompts, but do not take independent actions in the world. They provide outputs for humans to review and act upon.

Key characteristics of passive systems include:
- They respond only when prompted.
- They generate content, information, or predictions.
- They require human decision-making to implement recommendations.
- They do not modify external systems or data without explicit human approval.
- They have no persistent goals beyond responding to the current request.
- They operate in discrete interactions rather than continuous processes.

https://doi.org/10.1515/9783111583549-022

Foundation Models (like GPT-4), Expert Models with retrieval capabilities, content generation systems, predictive analytics dashboards, recommendation engines, and classification systems all fall into this category. Their outputs may be sophisticated, but there remains a human in the execution loop.

Agentic AI Systems

Agentic AI systems can observe their environment, make decisions, and take actions to achieve specified goals, often without immediate human intervention for each step. They have persistence across time and can adapt their strategies based on outcomes.

Key characteristics of agentic systems include:
– They can initiate actions based on goals or environmental triggers.
– They interact directly with other systems through APIs and integrations.
– They maintain context and persistence across time.
– They observe outcomes and adapt strategies based on results.
– They coordinate multiple steps to achieve defined objectives.
– They often operate in continuous feedback loops rather than discrete interactions.

Examples include autonomous trading systems, inventory management agents that can place orders, customer service agents that can issue refunds without human approval, scheduling assistants that can book appointments, and software development agents that can write and deploy code.

The Significance of Crossing the Boundary

The transition from passive to agentic implementation is not a minor technical change but a fundamental shift in how AI interacts with the world. This transition brings significant advantages in efficiency, responsiveness, and scalability. However, it also introduces new dimensions of risk that traditional AI governance frameworks often fail to address.

When agency is granted to AI systems, the buffer of human judgment—with its contextual awareness, ethical reasoning, and common sense—is removed from the execution path. Decisions translate directly into actions, often at speeds and scales beyond immediate human monitoring capabilities. This removal of the "human circuit breaker" represents a qualitative shift in risk profile, not merely a quantitative one.

16.2 Risk Amplification at the Action Boundary

When AI systems cross from generating information to taking action, several risk dimensions expand significantly.

The Risk Amplification Effect

Passive AI systems, which generate information for human review, contain an inherent safeguard: human judgment stands between the AI's output and real-world consequences. When this barrier is removed in agentic systems, several risk dimensions expand dramatically.

First, errors can propagate faster and farther. While a passive system's mistaken analysis might be caught before implementation, an agentic system's error can trigger cascading actions across multiple systems before detection. Second, the timeline for correction compresses significantly—from days or hours to potentially seconds. Third, the scope of potential impact extends beyond information to physical operations, financial transactions, or customer-facing interactions.

Consider a financial services context: A passive investment analysis system that makes portfolio recommendations presents fundamentally different risks than an agentic trading system that executes transactions autonomously. Both may use similar analytical approaches, but they exist on opposite sides of the action boundary.

From Time to Reflect to Time to React

Perhaps the most significant transformation at the action boundary is temporal. With passive systems, humans typically have time to reflect, verify, and contextualize AI outputs before taking action. With agentic systems, the timeline collapses to reaction speed—often requiring automated safeguards rather than human oversight.

This compression of decision time creates several challenges:
- Meaningful human review becomes impractical for many operations.
- The burden shifts from reviewing outputs to designing robust guardrails.
- Organizations must anticipate failure modes in advance rather than catching them in review.
- Recovery must be designed into systems rather than relying on human intervention.

The shift from "time to reflect" to "time to react" fundamentally alters how risks must be managed, often requiring different governance structures and technical safeguards.

The Observability Challenge

Agentic systems also present unique challenges for monitoring and transparency. While passive systems produce discrete outputs that can be reviewed comprehensively, agentic systems take ongoing actions that may be difficult to track in their entirety. This problem compounds when multiple AI agents interact, creating a complex web of decisions and actions that no single human observer can fully comprehend.

The observability challenge requires new approaches to transparency, including:
– Robust logging of all actions and decision factors.
– Automatic anomaly detection and alerting.
– Clear traceability from goals to actions.
– Aggregated views of system behavior that highlight potential issues.

Without these mechanisms, agentic systems can develop problematic behaviors that remain hidden until they cause significant harm.

16.3 The Agentic Risk Assessment Matrix

Leaders should evaluate proposed agentic AI implementations across five critical dimensions to determine appropriate controls and oversight:

Impact Breadth: How many users, stakeholders, or systems could be affected?
– **Narrow:** Affects limited internal processes or individual users.
– **Moderate:** Impacts departments or customer segments.
– **Broad:** Potential effects across entire organizations or customer bases.
– **Extensive:** Could affect markets, industries, or public interests.

Financial Exposure: What level of financial resources does the system control?
– **Minimal:** No direct financial authority.
– **Limited:** Small transaction authority with clear limits.
– **Significant:** Substantial budget authority or resource allocation power.
– **Critical:** Major financial decision-making capability with organizational impact.

Autonomy Duration: How long does the system operate between human checkpoints?
– **Micro:** Seconds to minutes between human verification.
– **Limited:** Hours of autonomous operation.

- **Extended:** Days of independent operation.
- **Persistent:** Weeks or longer of autonomous execution.

Decision Reversibility: How easily can actions be undone if errors occur?
- **Immediate:** Actions can be instantly reversed without consequence.
- **Recoverable:** Reversible with some effort but minimal lasting impact.
- **Difficult:** Requires significant intervention to correct.
- **Permanent:** Creates irreversible changes or commitments.

Verification Transparency: How observable are the system's actions and reasoning?
- **Transparent:** All decisions and actions are automatically logged with clear reasoning.
- **Traceable:** Actions are logged but reasoning requires analysis.
- **Partially Opaque:** Some actions or reasoning may not be fully visible.
- **Black Box:** Limited visibility into actions or decision processes.

16.4 Control Frameworks by Risk Level

Based on an organization's assessment across these dimensions, different levels of control become appropriate:

Baseline Controls (For all agentic systems)
- Clear role definition with explicit authority boundaries.
- Comprehensive logging of all actions taken.
- Regular performance audits against expected outcomes.
- Circuit breakers for automatic suspension under anomalous conditions.

Enhanced Controls (For moderate-risk agents)
- Human approval requirements for decisions above defined thresholds.
- Real-time monitoring dashboards with alert mechanisms.
- Regular simulation testing with adversarial scenarios.
- Explicit failover mechanisms to human operators.

Stringent Controls (For high-risk agents)
- Multi-level approval workflows for consequential actions.
- Shadow mode operation periods before full autonomy.
- Continuous parallel verification by separate oversight systems.
- Regular third-party audits of operation and outcomes.
- Time-limited authority with explicit renewal requirements.

16.5 Case Example: Financial Service Automation

Consider two different applications in financial services:

Scenario A: Passive Financial Analysis AI
- Generates investment recommendations for wealth managers.
- Analyzes market trends and portfolio performance.
- Suggests asset allocations based on client profiles.
- *Key distinction:* Humans review all recommendations before implementation.

Scenario B: Agentic Trading System
- Executes trades autonomously based on market conditions.
- Rebalances portfolios without per-transaction approval.
- Responds to market events in milliseconds.
- *Key distinction:* Takes financial actions without immediate human review.

While both systems might use similar underlying models, the agentic trading system requires substantially more robust controls. Its assessment might show:
- Impact Breadth: Moderate (affects specific client portfolios).
- Financial Exposure: Significant (controls substantial assets).
- Autonomy Duration: Micro (though cumulative decisions matter).
- Decision Reversibility: Difficult (market trades create permanent commitments).
- Verification Transparency: Partially Opaque (complex decision chains).

This profile would suggest implementing enhanced or stringent controls, including explicit trading limits, multi-layered oversight, comprehensive audit trails, and possibly parallel verification systems that flag unusual patterns for human review.

16.6 The Organizational Readiness Component

A final consideration in this risk framework is organizational readiness—whether the institution has the capabilities to effectively oversee agentic systems. This includes:
- Technical monitoring infrastructure.
- Clear escalation pathways.
- Response protocols for agent failures.
- Staff trained in agent supervision.
- Regular simulation exercises.

Organizations should match their agentic AI ambitions to their oversight maturity. Those with limited experience should begin with narrower agent authority and more restrictive controls, expanding only as their governance capabilities mature.

By systematically evaluating these risk dimensions before deployment, organizations can make informed decisions about where and how to deploy agentic AI while maintaining appropriate safeguards. The goal isn't to prevent innovation, but to ensure that as AI systems gain greater autonomy, their oversight frameworks evolve in parallel.

16.7 Bridging Technical and Organizational Controls

Technical safeguards alone are insufficient for managing agentic AI risks. Organizations must implement complementary governance structures that bridge technical and human oversight.

Balanced Control Systems

Effective governance of agentic AI requires balancing three types of controls:
- **Preventive Controls:** Guardrails that constrain what actions the agent can take.
- **Detective Controls:** Monitoring systems that identify problematic behaviors.
- **Corrective Controls:** Mechanisms to rapidly address issues once detected.

Too often, organizations focus primarily on preventive controls while neglecting detection and correction. This creates brittle systems that operate safely within narrow parameters but fail catastrophically when they encounter edge cases. A balanced approach ensures that even when prevention fails, detection and correction can mitigate harm.

Organizational Structure for Agent Oversight

Agentic AI requires clear lines of responsibility that often cut across traditional organizational boundaries. Three key roles should be established:
- **Business Owners:** Responsible for defining agent objectives and success metrics.
- **Technical Stewards:** Responsible for implementation, monitoring, and ongoing maintenance.
- **Risk Overseers:** Independent evaluators who assess safety, compliance, and ethical considerations.

These roles should have clear documentation, escalation paths, and decision authority. Without this clarity, risks can fall through organizational cracks, with technical teams assuming business leaders are providing oversight while business leaders assume technical safeguards are sufficient.

16.8 The Path Forward: Progressive Agency

The transition from passive to agentic AI need not be binary. Organizations can adopt a progressive approach that gradually increases autonomy as confidence and capabilities mature.

The Agency Ladder

Consider implementing a structured progression of increasing agency:
1. **Recommendation Mode:** The system suggests actions for human approval.
2. **Shadow Mode:** The system makes decisions but requires human confirmation before execution.
3. **Supervised Autonomy:** The system acts independently for routine cases but escalates exceptions.
4. **Bounded Autonomy:** The system operates independently within well-defined parameters.
5. **Full Autonomy:** The system has broad discretion with minimal human involvement.

Each step up this ladder should require formal evaluation, documented performance metrics, and explicit approval from both business and risk stakeholders.

Continuous Evaluation

Unlike passive systems that can be evaluated primarily on output quality, agentic systems require ongoing assessment of both their decisions and their impacts. Key evaluation mechanisms include:
– Performance dashboards that track key metrics in real-time.
– Regular reviews by cross-functional teams.
– Structured escalation of unusual patterns or outlier events.
– Periodic audits by independent specialists.

These evaluation practices should be embedded in the operational cadence of the organization, not treated as one-time assessments.

16.9 Conclusion: Agency as Responsibility

The transition from passive to agentic AI marks a fundamental shift in risk profile that demands corresponding changes in governance. When organizations deploy AI systems that can act in the world, they accept a new form of responsibility that extends beyond traditional software deployment.

This responsibility requires:

– Systematic assessment of risk dimensions specific to agentic systems.
– Tiered control frameworks that match safeguards to risk levels.
– Organizational structures that clarify oversight responsibilities.
– Progressive approaches that build confidence through measured steps.

By recognizing the action boundary as a critical threshold and implementing appropriate governance on both sides, organizations can harness the efficiency and scalability of agentic AI while maintaining appropriate safeguards. The frameworks presented in this chapter provide a foundation for that governance—one that acknowledges both the tremendous potential of autonomous systems and the unique risks they introduce.

As AI continues to evolve from passive advisor to active participant, our approach to risk must evolve with it. The organizations that succeed will be those that balance ambition with prudence, leveraging the power of agentic systems while building the governance structures needed to deploy them responsibly.

Bibliography

Antorini, Yun Mi, Albert M. Muniz, and Tormod Askildsen (2012). Collaborating with customer communities: Lessons from the LEGO Group. *MIT Sloan Management Review* 53(3), 73–80.

Bresnahan, Timothy F. and Manuel Trajtenberg (1995). General purpose technologies 'Engines of growth'? *Journal of Econometrics* 65(1), 83–108.

Brynjolfsson, Erik, Daniel Rock, and Chad Syverson (2019). Artificial intelligence and the modern productivity paradox. In *The Economics of Artificial Intelligence: An Agenda*, pp. 23–57.

Cemri, Mert, et al. (2025). Why do multi-agent LLM systems fail? arXiv:2503.13657.

David, Paul A. (1990). The dynamo and the computer: An historical perspective on the modern productivity paradox. *The American Economic Review* 80(2), 355–361.

Denning, Peter J. and Craig H. Martell (2015). *Great Principles of Computing*. Cambridge: MIT Press.

Hienerth, Christoph, Christopher Lettl, and Peter Keinz (2014). Synergies among producer firms, lead users, and user communities: The case of the LEGO producer–user ecosystem. *The Journal of Product Innovation Management* 31(4), 848–866.

IBM Research (Nov. 2024). What is retrieval-augmented generation (RAG)? Accessed: April 27, 2025. https://research.ibm.com/blog/retrieval-augmented-generation-RAG.

Krizhevsky, Alex, Ilya Sutskever, and Geoffrey E. Hinton (2012). Imagenet classification with deep convolutional neural networks. In: *Advances in Neural Information Processing Systems* 25.

Lewis, Patrick, et al. (2020). Retrieval-augmented generation for knowledge-intensive NLP tasks. In: *Advances in Neural Information Processing Systems* 33, pp. 9459–9474.

Madaan, Aman, et al. (2023). Self-refine: Iterative refinement with self-feedback. In: *Advances in Neural Information Processing Systems* 36, pp. 46534–46594.

Mancini, Jeannine (2024). Jeff Bezos says Amazon has had 'plenty of practice' with failure but believes it is 'the best place in the world to fail'. Yahoo Finance Web. Accessed: 2025-04-15. https://finance.yahoo.com/news/jeff-bezos-says-amazon-had-170926395.html.

McCulloch, Warren S. and Walter Pitts (1943). A logical calculus of the ideas immanent in nervous activity. *The Bulletin of Mathematical Biophysics* 5, 115–133.

Minsky, Marvin and Seymour Papert (1969). *Perceptrons: An Introduction to Computational Geometry*. Cambridge, MA: MIT Press.

von Neumann, John (2021). First draft of a report on the EDVAC, In: Harry R. Lewis (ed.), *Ideas that Created the Future: Classic Papers of Computer Science* 10, pp. 89–106. MIT Press. Chap. 10. Originally published in 1945.

Ng, Andrew (2024). Andrew Ng explores the rise of AI agents and agentic reasoning | BUILD 2024 Keynote. YouTube video. Accessed: 2025-04-15. https://www.youtube.com/watch?v=KrRD7r7y7NY.

Perrow, Charles (2011). *Normal Accidents: Living with High Risk Technologies*, updated edition. Princeton University Press.

Rawte, Vipula, Amit Sheth, and Amitava Das (2023). A survey of hallucination in large foundation models. arXiv:2309.05922.

Rosenblatt, Frank (1958). The perceptron: A probabilistic model for information storage and organization in the brain. *Psychological Review* 65(6), 386.

Rumelhart, David E., Geoffrey E. Hinton, and Ronald J. Williams (1986). Learning representations by back-propagating errors. *Nature* 323(6088), 533–536. https://doi.org/10.1038/323533a0

Samuel, Arthur L. (1959). Some studies in machine learning using the game of checkers. *IBM Journal of Research and Development* 3(3), 210–229.

https://doi.org/10.1515/9783111583549-023

Schrage, Michael (1999). *Serious Play: How the World's Best Companies Simulate to Innovate*. Harvard Business Press.

Schrage, Michael (2014). *The Innovator's Hypothesis: How Cheap Experiments Are Worth More Than Good Ideas*. MIT Press.

Solow, Robert (1987). We'd better watch out. *New York Times Book Review* 36.

von Hippel, Eric (2005). Democratizing innovation: The evolving phenomenon of user innovation. *Journal für Betriebswirtschaft* 55, 63–78.

von Hippel, Eric, Stefan Thomke, and Mary Sonnack (1999). Creating breakthroughs at 3M. *Harvard Business Review* 77(5), 47–57.

Werbos, Paul J. (1974). Beyond regression: New tools for prediction and analysis in the behavioral sciences. PhD thesis. Cambridge, MA: Harvard University.

Yao, Shunyu, et al. (2023). React: Synergizing reasoning and acting in language models. In: *International Conference on Learning Representations (ICLR)*.

List of Figures

https://doi.org/10.1515/9783111583549-024

List of Tables

https://doi.org/10.1515/9783111583549-025

Index

https://doi.org/10.1515/9783111583549-026